Why You're Still Single

Could it be that:

- YOU'RE KNOCKING YOURSELF OUT OF THE GAME

- YOU'RE JUST NOT THAT INTO YOURSELF

- YOU'RE BEING A BITCH

- YOU KNOW HOW TO BE THE *GIRL FRIEND*, BUT NOT THE *GIRLFRIEND*

- YOU'RE THE PATRON SAINT OF LOST CAUSES

- YOU FIGHT LIKE A GIRL

- YOU'RE BORING HIM IN THE BEDROOM

- YOU'RE MISSING THE SIGNALS FOR WHEN TO GET OUT . . . AND WHEN TO STICK AROUND

Evan and Linda have a different approach for you.

Also by Evan Marc Katz

I Can't Believe I'm Buying This Book:
A Commonsense Guide to Successful Internet Dating

Why You're Still Single

things your friends would tell you if you promised not to get mad

EVAN MARC KATZ
and LINDA HOLMES

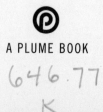

A PLUME BOOK

PLUME
Published by Penguin Group
Penguin Group (USA) Inc., 375 Hudson Street, New York, New York 10014, U.S.A.
Penguin Group (Canada), 90 Eglinton Avenue East, Suite 700, Toronto, Ontario,
Canada M4P 2Y3 (a division of Pearson Penguin Canada Inc.)
Penguin Books Ltd., 80 Strand, London WC2R 0RL, England
Penguin Ireland, 25 St. Stephen's Green, Dublin 2, Ireland
(a division of Penguin Books Ltd.)
Penguin Group (Australia), 250 Camberwell Road, Camberwell, Victoria 3124,
Australia (a division of Pearson Australia Group Pty. Ltd.)
Penguin Books India Pvt. Ltd., 11 Community Centre,
Panchsheel Park, New Delhi – 110 017, India
Penguin Books (NZ), cnr Airborne and Rosedale Roads, Albany,
Auckland 1310, New Zealand (a division of Pearson New Zealand Ltd.)
Penguin Books (South Africa) (Pty.) Ltd., 24 Sturdee Avenue, Rosebank,
Johannesburg 2196, South Africa

Penguin Books Ltd., Registered Offices: 80 Strand, London WC2R 0RL, England

First published by Plume, a member of Penguin Group (USA) Inc.

First printing, June 2006
10 9 8 7 6 5 4 3 2 1

Copyright © Evan Marc Katz and Linda Holmes, 2006
All rights reserved

℗ REGISTERED TRADEMARK—MARCA REGISTRADA

LIBRARY OF CONGRESS CATALOGING-IN-PUBLICATION DATA
Katz, Evan Marc.
    Why you're still single : things your friends would tell you if you promised not to
get mad / Evan Marc Katz & Linda Holmes.
        p.   cm.
    ISBN 0-452-28738-3 (trade pbk.)
    1. Single people—Psychology.   2. Single people—Attitudes.   3. Man-woman
relationships.   4. Dating (Social customs)   I. Holmes, Linda.   II. Title.
    HQ800.K35   2006
    646.7'7—dc22   2006000289

Printed in the United States of America
Set in Sabon

From Linda

*To my sister Susie. I don't remember ever
not liking you better than anyone.*

From Evan

*To my sister, Daryl. I've always said,
you got the good genes, kid.*

The definition of insanity is doing the same thing over and over and expecting different results.
　　　　　　　　　　　　　　　　　—Benjamin Franklin

Contents

Part III. You're Being a Bitch

Part IV. You Know How to Be the *Girl Friend*, but Not the *Girlfriend*

Part V. You're the Patron Saint of Lost Causes

Part VI. You Fight Like a Girl

Part VII. You're Boring Him in the Bedroom

Part VIII. You're Missing the Signals for When to Get Out . . . and When to Stick Around

Introduction

Evan

My name is Evan and I'm still single. I started writing this book because the titular question, which gets asked of anyone on the far side of thirty, can't summarily be dismissed in one line. Believe me, I've tried. Here was the best I could come up with to explain my perpetual bachelorhood: (1) I just haven't met the right women, and (2) I got dumped by the only two I would have married.

Yeah, well, both these statements are true and undoubtedly play a large part in why I'm still single. But so what? Acknowledging this doesn't put me any closer to my long-term goal of marriage. I can't force myself to meet "the right woman," and I can't go back and fix my past relationships. All I can do is look ahead.

Why You're Still Single is about looking ahead. But first we need to look back. We need to take stock of our past behavior and vow to act differently the next time around. Awareness doesn't mean you've found a quick fix, but it can certainly put you on the right path toward future success.

Being the authors of this book doesn't put us on a pedestal from which we will demonize you for being single. That would be horribly hypocritical, wouldn't it? No, Linda and I are two people who are going through it ourselves, who see a common thread connecting all of us, and who may just have something unique to say about the human condition. While most advice books pose facile answers to women about capturing a man to marry, we chose to ruminate on why 99 percent of relationships fail before they hit the altar. Not to mention the reasons why many of them don't get off the ground in the first place.

Just because we're spending all this time talking about how women trip themselves up doesn't mean we're not acutely aware of the issues surrounding the typical man. Alas, there's no point in writing a book that would weigh fourteen pounds, especially since there are only 8,317 men in America who would buy such a thing. If any of the other 150 million men are interested in changing, they're going to do it by their own volition. The moral of this story isn't that men are fine and women are broken, but rather that you can't change men and you can't make them read self-help books. All you can do is be aware of your own actions and try not to repeat the same mistakes over and over. After all, that would be insane, or so said a man who once flew a kite in a thunderstorm (apparently, any nut job can run around dispensing advice).

If knowledge is indeed power, we hope you feel empowered by what you're about to read. You deserve the best in life, and the only way to get it is to seek answers. We may not know for certain *why you're still single,* but we hope to stimulate some valuable conversation or, at the very least, get more laughs per page than *Poor Richard's Almanack.*

Linda

If you wander over to the cooking section in a bookstore, you won't find a cookbook called *Why You Burn Everything.* That's because you probably approach cooking pretty simply. When you look at yet another blackened grilled cheese sandwich you probably can't pass off as Cajun-style, you say, "It may be time to do something different." So you buy a book. It doesn't mean you're a bad person; it doesn't mean you have to like the book; it doesn't mean the people who wrote the book are smarter than you are; and it doesn't mean you have to do it that way if you don't want to. It means, "We've set off the smoke detector a few times ourselves over the years, and if you're looking for a different approach, we've got one."

Evan was already working on this book when we met, and when he described it to me, I believe my exact words were, "I *hate* those books." And I wasn't just being nice. For the most part, books for single women about being single—the members of the genre of *Building a Better Butterfly Net: Man-Catching Pointers for the Desperate, Miserable, Slowly Decaying Hag*—are insulting, condescending nonsense, shot through with sexist claptrap and a hundred other kinds of poison. They either suggest or flat-out declare that there's something fundamentally wrong with you if you're single (there isn't), that you can't be happy as a single person (you can), that single women have more things wrong with them than single men (they don't), or that *any* relationship is better than accursed spinsterhood (it's not—it's *really* not).

But there's a difference between beating yourself up and learning from mistakes you and everyone else have already made. There's nothing wrong with you because you can't cook, either. That doesn't mean that if you keep putting the same sandwich in the same pan on the same burner at the same setting and you leave it there for the same amount of time, it will eventually stop burning because you're a good, well-intentioned, deserving person. You may be great, but your dinner is still going to burn. You know this because you've done it. A lot. Your choices, as we see them, are to learn to like the taste of char, resolve to order takeout forever, or consider the possibility of doing something different.

It's not that you're single for every reason we're going to suggest. You're not picking fights *and* being jealous *and* being sexually timid *and* hanging on to past hurts *and* hung up on your looks. At least we hope you're not. But everything you're going to read about is something we've seen—in ourselves, in our friends, in relative strangers, and in all the stories that those people have told us over and over (and over) again. These are observations that hatched over beers, in e-mails to grieving friends, in pained conversations with people we want to date or are dating or have dated, or, occasionally, in the shower. We've done this stuff. We *are* this stuff.

So what do *we* know? Well, really, what does *anybody* know? Who *is* qualified to talk about the mysterious landscape of relationships between single men and single women? If it can't be single men because they don't know what it's like to be a single woman, and it can't be single women because they obviously don't know how to get a decent boyfriend, then what are you left with? People who haven't been single since Reagan was president? What if you wind up taking advice from someone whose marriage then goes belly up, or whose boyfriend you wouldn't choose over a chaste evening of Parcheesi and Diet 7UP? If the ability to collect relationships like Hummel figurines made a person brilliant about the subject, you'd be eagerly reading a relationship book called *Kisses, Dahlink!* by the Gabor sisters. I mean, fourteen husbands! An even twenty if you count Magda. They must *really* know what they're doing.

In the end, everyone's experiences are irrelevant to you, and everyone's experiences are universal. You're not going to know whether the things Evan and I say make sense because they got us dates, or laid, or married. You're going to know whether they make sense because you're going to read them for yourself, and if you're anything like us, you're going to recognize yourself and your friends. And maybe even the Gabor sisters.

This book isn't about catching men or reeling anybody in.

Catching is for escaped zoo animals and nine-year-olds playing freeze tag, and reeling is for trout. This is about you considering the possibility that you're tripping over your own feet—no matter how much of an amazing, smart, hot, totally worthwhile ass-kicker you may be as a general rule. In other words: If you're looking for a different approach, we've got one.

PART I

You're Knocking Yourself Out of the Game

Do I Want to Date Right Now?
I Don't Know, Maybe . . .

The Desperation Tango

Women Who Hate Men Who
Hate Women

1

Do I Want to Date Right Now?
I Don't Know, Maybe . . .

If you're not committed to getting this thing right, putting in the necessary effort to meet men, and bouncing back each time something goes wrong, you're not a good candidate for a partner. All that talk about relationships being hard? It's true.

Evan

We've all been on the rebound. Whether you're the dumper or the dumpee, the aftermath of a failed relationship is rarely pretty. And then there's the rebound timetable. When is it okay to get back out there? When have you healed enough to start meeting people again without making your next date into your next victim? No one can blame a woman who's coming off a string of rocky breakups for sitting it out on the sideline for a period of time. But (there's always a "but") you do need to leave your house eventually. Sure, "a good man *is* hard to find," but that statement ceases to mean anything when you add the corollary, "especially if you never leave your cats and your TiVo in your godforsaken apartment."

Fact: If you're more concerned with Brad and Angelina's love life than you are with your own, you're not that interested in meeting a guy. And you don't have to be a hermit or a couch potato to put up walls. Spend sixty hours a week at work? Hard to meet a guy there. Love hanging out with your close girlfriends and their cool husbands? Not too many single guys in their babies' playroom. Embarrassed about going to singles events? Lots of people aren't. Even if it just means reading an issue of *People* magazine at a local coffee shop, being out in the world increases your chances of meeting someone exponentially—if only because the chances of meeting someone at home are, like, zero.

I'm not saying it's easy. This is a universal dilemma—especially as people get further entrenched into their single lives. You're over the bar scene. You have mortgage payments. You have more responsibility at work. Your friends are coupled off and reproducing like rabbits. Somehow, life is not a dream, and it certainly isn't following the scripts of all the Meg Ryan movies that you own on DVD. In fact, this movie sucks so bad that you're thinking of asking for your money back.

Yeah, it's tough out there, but it's tough on everyone. And if you look at the people who are happy, the people whose lives you envy, the people that you'd like to be one day, you'll quickly realize that the difference between contentment and discontent is the feeling of connection. Just a hunch, but Mariah Carey isn't having breakdowns because she doesn't feel attractive, because she doesn't have money, or because she can't meet a man who's interested in her. My guess is that she, and dozens of other celebrities who turn to drink and drugs and bad fashion, are supremely sad because, no matter where you are or what you do, it's freakin' lonely out there. The desire for partnership knows no class boundaries. Although a C-List marriage stands a better chance of lasting than an A-List Marriage. Thank you, *People* magazine.

Sometimes it's hard to accept that Mr. Right doesn't know you exist. He doesn't have your address. He doesn't know where you work. He's not going to knock on your door and tell you that he's heard great things about you and that maybe you could grab a drink sometime. So until you put yourself out into the world with your "Single and Looking (But Not Desperately)" placard, you're screwed. Do men like a challenge? Sure we do. But there's a difference between a guy making the effort to get your number at a charity event and a guy making the effort to ask for your number by breaking into your office at 10 P.M. while you're still working.

Ladies, please don't make us commit crimes to meet you. Just come out and play once in a while.

Linda

MY APARTMENT IS NOT GODFORSAKEN, AND I DO NOT HAVE CATS.

Did Evan's section of this chapter make you feel a little . . . defensive? Yeah, me too. It's not that I doubt that these things are true. I have, as Evan points out, never met a guy in my apartment (probably a good thing, because a guy you stumble upon while he's rifling through your underwear drawer for expensive jewelry is unlikely to be a good prospect).

It's also true that somewhere around thirty, I hit a point where my social plans were substantially impaired by the fact that everybody had spouses and in-laws and babies to contend with. Worse yet, I had built up a network of friends I loved who were scattered from New York to California. My friends were great, but they weren't around much to actually do anything. Besides, I got busy with multiple jobs and things I wanted to do, and I didn't have as much hanging-around time either.

But the entire time, I was, overall, getting happier and happier. I think the defensiveness a lot of single women feel about stereotypes of bonbon-popping comes from being asked to disown their entire lives—to subscribe to a brand of pathos that, to their credit, they don't feel. I wouldn't trade my absent friends for a passel of hovering, out-every-Saturday-night, Anistonian/Schwimmerific locals for any amount of money, no matter how depressing weekend television is. You're not obligated to feel defensive about spending Saturday night at home. You're entitled to like your life as it is. In fact, you *should* like your life as it is. What about those people who think being on your own makes you a charity case, people who think it means you have nothing, people who think the only reason you can be at home alone is that you've attempted to make plans with everyone you can think of and everyone has said no? These people are fools, and every one of them can walk right off the plank of the S.S. *Spinsterhood*, as far as I'm concerned.

You can have a great life, great friends, a satisfying career, a close family, serious aspirations, and no time or inclination to sit around in footy pajamas listening to the Carpenters. Your apartment is still a bad place to meet men, just like mine is. And so is your married friends' living room, and so is your workplace in many cases, and so is the grocery store if you're tearing through it in ten minutes on your way from the office to the gym.

Ultimately, it's about making room in your life and your schedule for the things you want to happen. Because when you find yourself lamenting that something *hasn't* happened, it makes sense to wonder whether you've arranged your life so as to prevent it. If you're not putting yourself in a position to meet anyone, it's not about whether that's a black mark on your record, or whether it makes you pitiable, or whether it negates what a great friend or artist or basketball player you are. It's about the fact that you have choices, and you make them one way or the other, every day. If they're working in direct opposition to everything you want, you might want to reconsider the way you're living your life.

2

The Desperation Tango

The more you run at the men you meet like you have five minutes to impress them because you hate being single and you must get married soon, the more some of them are going to freak out. It's hard to be all Zen about it, but you kind of have to.

Evan

I have a friend who is a bit of a player, but deep down he wants to fall in love. Ironically, whenever he meets a woman he thinks could be a girlfriend, he completely loses his cool. Generally, that means downing an extra drink, confessing his kidlike excitement, and never hearing from her again. Is he a great guy? Yep. Is his heart in the right place? Uh-huh. Has he had any serious relationships recently? No way. The women he doesn't like all fall for him; the ones he falls for all disappear.

Clearly, desperation knows no gender boundaries. A screenwriter I know wanted to write a character based on the most desperate woman he'd ever met. Within three minutes of meeting him at a mutual friend's Thanksgiving dinner, she told him that she was on a quest to be married and have lots of babies as soon as possible. She was twenty-two. She didn't make a good subject; as is often the case, truth is stranger than fiction.

Like a child trying to hold a balloon tightly and inadvertently popping it, trying too hard to catch and keep a man is the one thing that is sure to drive him away. Simply the concept (and cottage industry) of landing a man is antithetical to your stated goal. Any man who allows himself to be landed by a woman on a mission is probably one not worth landing. I, for one, wouldn't want to go out with

a woman who wears her ticking clock around her neck like Flavor
Flav. "Yeah, boyyyyyyyy. Wanna marry me?" Uh, no, thanks. But
the next guy in line shakes hands like a Vulcan, so maybe he's interested.

As stated earlier, the whole man-sweeping-you-off-your-feet
thing is impossible if you're lodged on your couch with a stack of
work under one arm and Chinese takeout in the other. And despite
what all those anachronistic guides tell you about never introduc-
ing yourself to guys, they're wrong. Not only that, but they're
dangerous. Are you going to tell me that a confident woman can't
make eye contact with a guy, write him a quick note online, or
start up a conversation at a bar? Puh-leeze. Men only get turned
off when a woman's outgoing nature looks more like desperation
than it does like confidence. And what does desperation look
like?

- Calling him four consecutive times before he calls you back.
- Dropping plans with your friends just to go out with him.
- Bringing up your ticking clock on a date before you even
  know if he likes you.
- Telling a guy at a Thanksgiving dinner that you *will* be
  married—although you don't know the groom's name yet—
  by the time you meet again next year.

Go out with a guy and tell him sincerely at the end of a fabu-
lous date, "I'm so glad to have you in my life," and he won't be in
your life. Show up at his house with a handwritten note explaining
how excited you are that you met, and watch him flee. Push for a
commitment before it seems organic just because you're working
on an accelerated baby-related timetable? You don't need me to tell
you what will happen. Sincere expressions of excitement are great
when you're on the same page, but until you're sure that he's just
as excited as you are, it's probably smart to put a lid on it.

Linda

The upside to choosing desperation as the theme of your single-dom is that it's always possible that some compassionate soul will come along and pity your existence so thoroughly that he will fasten upon, woo, and marry you when he otherwise wouldn't have given you the time of day. And years later, when people ask him what drew him to you, he will place his hand over his pacemaker and say, "It was all the weeping and the gnashing of teeth." It'll all be very romantic, really. Happy retirement!

The downside, unfortunately, is everything else. Seriously. *Everything* else. It's not that everyone hasn't felt needy from time to time. I've certainly been known to come home from a horrific day with a hangnail and an ugly snarl, thinking to myself, "I would literally pay five thousand dollars right now if someone would make me dinner and let me lie on the couch with my feet in his lap." (I realize I may have just invented a new form of high-profit, low-risk prostitution. Please don't beat me to the patent office.) It can feel . . . well, yeah, "desperate" is it.

Problem number one: This is not an attractive quality. You know this if you have ever been hit on by a desperate person. He comes up to you with whatever weird-ass come-on he's chosen, and it's like he's holding up a sign. A sign that says ANYONE WILL DO. In crayon. Your eyes narrow, you look at the bottom of the sign, and you see that it has two more words on it: EVEN YOU. And that's when you make a face, because you can't feel particularly thrilled or flattered about being approached by someone who makes it clear that you're the last best option, which is the impression created by that needy, hungry, urgent, gasping thing.

Problem number two: An overwhelming sense of urgency vastly increases the likelihood that you will fuck up. Did you ever play Pitfall!? In the olden days, when I was a girl, before PlayStation 2, there was Atari, and there was Pitfall! In this particular game, you had to run your little guy through the jungle, hopping on crocodile heads and swinging on ropes and whatnot. It wasn't a very hard game, provided you weren't in too much of a hurry. Particularly with the croc heads, it was critical to slow down. Because if you didn't and you tried to just fly through the thing as fast as possible, you'd fuck up and you'd fall in the water or be eaten. The point I'm making is that if you're bolting through your single life just trying like hell to find some way out of it before you turn thirty, or thirty-five, or forty, or whatever age you've arbitrarily chosen, you are going to wind up married to a crocodile head.

It's not hard to rattle off the entirely understandable pressures that can bring this whole mess on—you can start with the potentially soul-crushing biological clock issue that has a way of sucking the fun out of patiently going with the flow the way you otherwise would. But that's only the most well-known example. There's also watching the cake-cutting at the wedding of your last friend to get married. There's being the only single person left in your family except the cousin who's in jail, leaving you to spend every major holiday throwing off the seating arrangements by making all the even numbers odd. There's the overwhelming sexual frustration that arises when you have already dated and broken up with the shower massage twice. And, of course, there's just wanting somebody to let you put your damn feet in his damn lap because, *wow*, some days are long and it's not like you wouldn't reciprocate on another occasion, but, *wow*, did we mention how long some days are?

It's hard to relax. It's like the old saying about telling someone not to think about an elephant. The more you feel yourself trying to relax, the worse it gets, until you've got yourself twisted into a neurotic little knot, and then you *really* can't get a date because who wants to go out with a neurotic little knot?

The solution? It's not going to help to whistle a happy tune and pretend not to be desperate. What's important is actually not to *be* desperate. Intense neediness is more of a stink than it is an affectation; if you're afflicted with it, you're probably not going to hide it very well. Filling your life with friends and work that's meaningful to you and whatever else pops your personal cork has the dual advantages of making you happier and making you more attractive. And the list of things that share those two critical advantages is short, indeed. It certainly doesn't include mascara or chocolate croissants.

Look at it this way: Nobody is going to want to jump into a life you can't wait to get the hell out of. It's like inviting people to a party already in progress by advertising that no one in attendance is having a good time. So don't go around holding up a sign that says you're dissatisfied with where you are. Nobody likes to be addressed in crayon anyway.

3

Women Who Hate Men
Who Hate Women

Everybody's got old scars, but if you wouldn't date the "women are bitches" guy (and you shouldn't), don't be the "men are pigs" woman.

Evan

Women are crazy. Insecure, irrational, emotional, conniving, jealous, catty, and petty.

Just kidding. But whether you believe any of the above stereotypes, you have to admit that there are a good number of men (and women) who do. Doesn't quite sound fair to the hundreds of millions of women who do not personify Evil Incarnate, does it?

Yet, somehow, all I could think of when I was talking to Linda about this chapter was, "Holy shit! Am I the 'women are crazy' guy?" My God, I think I am, and I'm embarrassed. Or at least I have been at times, enough to give me some insight into how somebody becomes that person—and can overcome it with a little perspective.

I'll save most of my personal material for the "Why *I'm* Still Single" tome, which will be bound in a series of Time-Life books after I go on my one-thousandth date in May 2012. But it's more than a little relevant, so bear with me. See, like many people, I have a history of dating women with issues: divorced parents, cheating boyfriends, body image problems—your standard fare. All were good people, but I could no longer bear to pay the price for the sins of the father, the exes, and *Maxim* magazine. Eventually, I made a decision not to date anyone like that ever again.

Since then, I have dated four women, and each one of them had it together—brains, beauty, kindness, warmth, you name it. The relationships ended for a variety of reasons—I wasn't right for them, they weren't right for me—but the point of the story is this: By being choosier about whom I dated, I struck gold. Retiring my troubled woman paradigm and finding the kind of level-headed woman I'd always desired, I learned that it wasn't women who sucked—it was my decision making.

As you have undoubtedly already ascertained, despite the fact that this book is for women, three-quarters of this stuff could just as easily apply to men. Frankly, I don't think men and women are from different planets at all—neighboring states perhaps, but more likely, we live right up the street, just out of shouting distance from you. This focus on our differences fails to explain what's universal about us: that the vast, vast majority of people are good at heart and just want to be loved for who they are. This yearning for connection is what drives us and sometimes steers our lives into a ditch. Consider that ditch your relationship with a Bad Man. And, witty self-help books notwithstanding, there's not a tow truck in sight to get you out. That's your job.

Since there is no magic remedy for the curse that is Men, all you can do is pick yourself up, consider the mistakes you've made in the past, and ask yourself who you'd rather spend time with. If it's the Duchess of Bitterville, you can have her, but I'll choose Miss Happy and Light every time.

Linda

When you've been through eight thousand variations of what my friend Sarah memorably refers to as That Guy, it's easy to wind up flat on your back in the tub, drinking a glass of wine against a backdrop of weepy torchsongs as you mutter, "Man, how does this keep *happening* to me?" And you drink. "I hate him." Drink. "And the last one, too. I hate them both." Drink. "And I'm not crazy about the one before that, either." Drink. Add more bubbles and more hot water. "It's all of them. I hate men."

That much is okay. When it's just you and your tub and your wine, there's no point in trying not to be angry and hurt. Cry, hit things, and don't bother giving yourself pep talks. But when that part is over, you're going to have to throw out the empty Kleenex box and drag yourself back to reality. And reality is that men do not, on any broad level, suck. They're not pigs, dogs, or chimps.

Believe me, I've heard it all. "They're less sensitive." Forget it. I've known men who instinctively know just what I need at the moment that I need it—whether this is the moment to tease me, to ask how I am, to kiss me on the forehead, or to tell me to stop being a big nutbar and shut up, all in a lovely, unobtrusive way that belies any tin ear you may have heard about. "They're not sentimental." This is a lie, too. I've seen guys make romantic gestures so perfectly formed that they would make you faint. The list goes on: "They can't talk about their feelings." "They're mean." "They're liars." No, no, and no. As many of these as you can set up, a smart woman can and will knock down.

But you don't even need to hear this, really, do you? Because if you didn't already know it, you wouldn't be looking for anyone. You'd stop going out, you'd choose to be single, and you'd be grateful that you figured it out before you found yourself inexorably intertwined with one of these horrible, horrible people.

You know it isn't true that men suck. And if you know it's not true, for God's sake, *stop saying it*. Everyone has been in the company of this woman—the one who always answers the "Why am I still single?" question in exactly this way. "I'm single because *men suck*," she will tell you. If you are this woman and this is your theory . . . well, not to stop you from sitting around at your pity party all day long tootling away on your plastic horn, but, honestly, knock it off.

It's time, in general, to get off the merry-go-round of men sitting around trash-talking women and women sitting around trash-talking men and show a little mercy to the human beings involved. Believe me, I've got one or two champs on my record: lying, vicious, cruel, manipulative, genuinely unsatisfactory human beings—none of which I discovered about them until it was too late, of course. It happens. But the hard truth is that those guys are long gone, and the *really* hard truth is that they're not thinking about me. People who do you wrong will, in many cases, get away with it, move on with their lives, and forget all about you. There's karmic justice, but it's certainly not as reliable or as speedy as we'd all like it to be, and sometimes you just have to go on without it.

Knowing that, you have one choice to make, and that's whether you're going to let all the worst guys you've ever known live rent-free in your head for the next twenty years, putting their grubby, ghostly fingers all over your relationships. If you're smart, you'll kick them out, and the only way to do that is to recognize that their behavior reflects only on them. They own all of it. They didn't inherit it along with their chromosomes, and they didn't learn it from a handbook given out in junior high. It's got nothing to do with the next guy, unless the next guy happens to also be a creep, and if that's the case, then it's time to consider the possibility that it's not an accident, and that . . . well, it may be your creep radar, and not the male species, that's on the fritz.

Furthermore, if the next guy is worth knowing, and you pull your "Woe is me, I'm so through with men" routine, he's going to spot it and know that what you really want is for him to prove you wrong. It's just another variation on the highly unattractive practice of telling a guy that if he really wants you, he'll have to talk you into it. Would you pick a guy who did that? Who expected you to take responsibility for proving that women aren't bitches? To clean up everything that's been spilled on him since the home-coming dance? That kind of rehab work on somebody else's head is a miserable, unending slog, and smart people don't sign up for it. You wouldn't, and the guys you want won't, either.

PART II

You're Just Not That into Yourself

Insecurity Kills More Relationships
Than Infidelity

———

Tip Your Baggage Handler

———

A Flexible Backbone

———

The Power of No

1

Insecurity Kills More Relationships Than Infidelity

Simply put, the more you love yourself, the more likely you are to be a good partner. If you have issues and project them onto the guy you're dating, you likely won't be dating him for long.

Evan

Whoever said "If you don't love yourself, you can't love anybody else" hit the nail on the head with a sledgehammer. *Everything* that goes wrong in a relationship can be attributed, in some form, to insecurity. Unfortunately, short of a scientific breakthrough that provides 100 mg of self-esteem in caplet, lozenge, or latte form, we're left to lament the sorry state of affairs that leaves so many people unequipped to be equal partners in a healthy, stable relationship. The question is not *why* people are insecure; the reasons are myriad, and for the sake of this exercise, it doesn't really matter. What I want to explore is *how* these insecurities can sabotage your romance.

If "being right" gets you nowhere and "winning is everything" means nothing, why is it so hard for us to shut our big yaps? Listen, I'm quite an authority on stupid arguments. Another thing I know from experience: Insecure people tell you what you're doing wrong; secure ones agree to disagree. Insecure people get jealous at the slightest whiff of flirting; secure people trust their significant others. Insecure people talk trash about their friends and try to take other people down; secure people don't see the value.

You're probably shaking your head, either in disagreement, or

...ne people who have to put up with this crap.
...i have a few friends who have turned their baggage
...ie else's problem. The question is whether you do as
...re's a simple quiz to find out:

Have you turned your baggage into someone else's problem?
Do you hash out every argument until there is a winner?
Do you make him apologize for having a different opinion,
    even if he has a reasonable justification for it?
Do you talk badly about your boyfriend behind his back?
Do you accuse everyone else of being insecure?

Score 100 points for every yes answer. Any score over 99 means
you might be insecure.

Then again, we're all insecure, so a better way to look at arguments of this sort is from his perspective. Put another way: Would
you want your boyfriend to exhibit any of these behaviors toward
you? Of course not.

Confident women aren't hung up on how they look in the
bedroom. They're not trying to convince you that you voted for
the wrong political party. They're not losing sleep about your old
sweater and how it reflects on them when you're out with
friends. This doesn't mean they don't have opinions or that they
blindly support everything their boyfriends do; it just means that
they're comfortable in their own skin. Their focus is on themselves, not on railing on others to compensate for their own personal dissatisfaction.

Self-esteem is the greatest gift of all, and I think world peace
could be achieved if people liked themselves enough to not be
cruel to each other. As you know, dealing with insecure men is an
awful task, but since there's nothing you can do about that, turn
your focus inward and try not to let all your crap end up on his
plate.

Linda

I nod at a lot of what Evan is saying, with one exception: It matters why—and to what degree—you're insecure. Because there's insecurity of the type that everyone has, and then there's insecurity of the type that's paralyzing, and you can't handle them the same way.

The first kind you can manage, sort of like a chronic illness. You treat the symptoms, you learn pain management, you hold the occasional telethon, all that good stuff. But if you think you've got the kind that's got you completely turned around, you're going to have to stop whatever else you're doing and pay attention to that until you can knock it down to a manageable size. It's no fun at all, ripping out your internal architecture. Therapy, journals . . . this is not a fun process. But you might have to do it because it's possible to feel so low that you'd never choose a decent person to get into a relationship with in the first place, and even if you miraculously managed to get through that part, you'd jump on the first reason to kill it. And if there weren't a reason, you'd create one.

But what about run-of-the-mill insecurity, which basically applies to everyone else? Reread everything Evan just told you. Twice. As far as I'm concerned, this is where it's at for the great majority of people who can't figure out what's going wrong. It's somewhere in here, in this swamp of self-doubt and self-denial and the secret belief that you're a fraud and everyone will eventually find out. Obviously, not every asshole is insecure, and it's probably the most pitifully overused excuse for unforgivable behavior in modern emotional life with the possible exception of blaming your parents. But it's a legitimate issue for an awful lot of people who are sincerely trying to forge good relationships and finding that they can't.

Even if these garden-variety insecurities can't be entirely chased away—and they probably can't—I do believe there are specific things you can do to chip away at them.

First: Everybody needs reassurance. But if you raise a specific point and you get satisfaction, *accept it*. One time, then out. Learn it. Practice it. *One time, then out*. If you ask the guy whether he's mad at you, and he says no? Take him at his word. The likelihood that he's messing with you and actually *is* mad and the right thing to do is to keep asking until he admits it may be greater than zero, but it is *very small* compared to the likelihood that he's not mad now but will be if you don't let it go. Play the odds. If you're not willing to play the odds that he's *not* messing with you, then that's an excellent sign that he's not the right guy for you.

Second: Learn to take a compliment. I'm a little weak in this area myself, but the least you can do is to be conscious of it. If you're squeamish and instinctively (1) play it off; (2) try to blunt it by volleying back an even bigger compliment; or, and I cannot stress this one enough, (3) question the compliment's sincerity because it otherwise embarrasses you, that's just rude. Again, this sort of nonsense isn't insecurity itself so much as it is an echo of it, but you have to start somewhere. And even if it takes a while to knock it off, suck it up and keep trying.

Third: No matter how much you think insecurity is the root cause of your less attractive behaviors, don't haul it out as an excuse. It's easy to think of yourself as a victim of insecurity, like it's a natural disaster you've gone through all alone. Like you're and a poster child for your own little Red Cross relief effort. Poor you. But the fact that you pick fights, or you're jealous and possessive, or you're cutting and mean—those things aren't any less toxic to your relationships or any less painful to other people just because you're able to tag them as things you do because you're insecure. The guy didn't make you insecure; you can't ask him to pay the bill for that. (If he *is* the reason you're insecure? Again, *wrong guy*.) Willingness to take responsibility for your own behavior, and to accept the fact that you'll have to change it if you expect it to change, is one of the biggest differences between happy and unhappy people. So you're insecure. So what? So's your boyfriend. Everybody's insecure. It's not a "get out of jail free" card.

Ultimately, it is very easy to say that you should overcome your insecurities, but it's very difficult to do. Your nonsense is always with you. It's not about pretending you don't have it, and it's not about apologizing for it constantly. I think it's about finding somebody who can live with it, and whose nonsense you can live with, and then trying really hard not to dump it all over each other. I realize that this, as a romantic fantasy, is not up there with schlepping a shoe all over the kingdom until you find one magical foot, but it's all I've got.

2

Tip Your Baggage Handler

Repeat this to yourself one thousand times: Screwed-up people are not more interesting than people with their heads together. Baggage is not fascinating, romantic, or exciting. It is very, very tiring. Men who are polite and emotionally mature are hot. Learn it, love it, live by it.

Evan

Apparently, many intelligent women prefer a man with emotional complexity, even if it means that he can be verbally abusive, inaccessible, and generally loonier than Courtney Love on a bender. Now, I can't speak for all men, but while I may have tolerated similar behavior, I can't say I've ever preferred it. Anytime I found myself dating a woman who was an emotional roller coaster, the only reason I stuck with her was because I was lonely and her presence in my life helped to fill a void. Either that, I was getting the best sex of my life. Lame, but true.

Put another way: Could you ever picture a man saying out loud, "There's something that's just so mysterious about her. Sometimes I look in her eyes and I feel like she totally understands me, and other times I have no idea what she's thinking. She runs really hot and cold, but I can't get enough of her. I think I'm going to stick around until I can crack her shell. One day she'll learn to be more emotionally available and loving." Let's be honest, tolerance for female ambivalence is not a stereotypically male attribute.

Women tend to see more nuance in every scenario, so it's no surprise that they give undeserving men the benefit of the doubt. But what for? Haven't most women since the beginning of time had a thing for jerks and realized at some point that jerks were always going to be jerks?

I was the nice guy in high school who enjoyed being friends with cute girls who wouldn't go out with me in a million years. I figured, *If that's as close as I can get, I'll take it. Maybe one day they'll realize what I'm worth.* Okay, maybe that was my parents talking, but the point is that I would listen to boy problems galore—essentially, nice girls being treated like crap by assholes with good looks and C averages—and not once did any of these girls ever say, "Hmm, Evan's a great guy with a really kick-ass mullet. I'll bet he'd be a wonderful boyfriend." After one three-hour counseling session with a hot girlfriend, I couldn't contain myself. I asked her what it was about me that made her think of me as just a friend. The answer, predictably, was, "I don't know. I want to date a guy just like you. But not you." So there's your nice-guy story for you.

But it's not simply the rejection of the nice guy that's keeping so many women single. It's the *acceptance of the screwed-up guy*. Because screwed-up guys draw screwed-up women into a whole "Misery Loves Company" episode of *Love Connection*—where both parties are brought together not by the audience but by their insecurities and inadequacies. Women who have their shit together simply don't have the patience for the screwed-up guy.

Admittedly, there are a few people who probably enjoy the histrionics and the moods and the makeup sex that come with dating drama kings and queens. But I'd bet that most are just willing to tolerate the drama because, thus far, that drama comes attached to the "best" person they could find. Essentially, they're saying, "Yeah, he's inconsistent, selfish, and distant, but he's all mine." One in the Prozac-swilling hand is worth two in the chain-smoking bush, I suppose. Just realize that every second you're spending with the wrong guy is a second that you're not out looking for the right one—the guy who gives, the guy who listens, the guy who learns.

Linda

I have no idea whom to blame for the romantic mythology surrounding brooding, emotionally limited, narcissistic yahoos. I'm tempted to chalk it up to movies where selfish jerks are eventually revealed to be wounded birds of some sort. Or it might be the uglier side of the therapy culture, which sells the idea that self-destructive (or just destructive) behavior usually has some secondary cause to the point where it transforms those same selfish jerks into challenges and tempts you with the idea that they might be amenable to a solution, like crossword puzzles.

For whatever reason, a surprising number of women are attracted to what is, for want of a gentler expression, bullshit. Guys who can't commit, who can't relate, who can't get along with anyone, who can't tell the truth . . . these guys get a lot of action; especially when they're young. If you don't believe me, find the nearest guy who *isn't* like this, and ask him whether he's ever seen it. He'll probably clench his teeth so hard he'll break a filling because, in my experience, that's how frustrating normal guys find this phenomenon.

It's not that women really want jerks, exactly. I think it's a matter of mistaking emotional clutter for emotional complexity. Here's an analogy: Imagine a messy apartment. There's an incredible quantity of stuff lying around: books in tall stacks, Chinese food containers in the corners, DVDs in and out of boxes scattered around the TV . . . the place is in chaos. And while you wouldn't really want to live there, there might be some part of you that would look around and grudgingly admit, "There's a lot going on here." Now, imagine the same apartment after somebody has cleaned it up. The books are on the shelves, the trash is thrown away, the DVDs are alphabetized. This is a much nicer place to live. But it's a little . . . you know, boring. And that's in spite of the fact that the same books are being read, the same food is being eaten, and the same DVDs are being watched. You're just in the presence of a person who knows how to clean up after himself.

Let me tell you something about the guys I know who are emotionally mature: They have just as much going on as everyone else. Their histories are often just as complicated, if not more so. The ranks of the healthy and rational include plenty of guys who have been in rehab, or been divorced, or seen their parents' marriages end horribly, or had their own dreams thwarted in some ugly way—all the things that creeps are fond of waving around as explanations for why they lie or cheat on you or generally continue to be creeps.

The difference is that the healthy and rational people have at least undertaken the process of digesting that baggage and placing it in some sort of perspective so that it doesn't have to become your problem. They know from suffering just as much as the chain-smoking turtlenecks who sit around brooding into their beers and writing free verse and dragging everyone else into their little theater of agony. The sane ones are still working on their crap, too. Who isn't? The difference is that they're not fetishizing their own misery or asking you to embrace it as a permanent condition. And that's a benefit to you because the only thing you can guarantee yourself about that kind of hair-pulling drama is that if you cuddle up next to it, it'll get on you.

In the end, you just have to stop assuming that men who prove over and over again that they can't cope on their own are that way because they feel things extra deeply. That isn't why they're like that. They're not behaving this way because they've discovered new frontiers of personal growth. They're just not dealing. It's not romantic or powerful; it's clichéd and a little spineless.

You're going to get plenty of emotional complications from *anyone*. Even people who have their lives very well pulled together have their share of problems and will give you a lot of opportunities to practice patience and understanding. There's no point in starting out with someone who isn't even trying.

3

A Flexible Backbone

Don't mistake self-esteem for fear of guys who don't encourage and enable all your crap. Finding that line between the delight of a person who genuinely challenges you and the misery of a person who doesn't think very highly of you isn't always easy. Do it anyway.

Evan

The most common, and perhaps most logical, reaction to being mistreated is to settle on a guy who treats you like a queen. And although it may not be the worst problem in the world, there's definitely a point when his being good to you actually becomes bad for you.

To broaden my perspective in this chapter, I did a little more "research" (i.e., talking to strange women in a coffee shop one rainy Sunday afternoon). Here are some of the quotes that I culled from the anonymous subjects on men who indulge their every whim:

- "It's disenchanting when a man kisses your ass. I may not want to initiate all the phone calls, but I definitely don't want to be someone's entire world."
- "It's pathetic if a guy puts his life on hold when he barely knows you. Sometimes guys seem to get more excited about the idea of the person than the actual person."
- "Devotion is nice but only if you're in a relationship of equals. Otherwise, it sings of desperation."

Got it. So if it's so annoying, why would you ever date guys like this?

Everyone seemed to agree that the main reason to date an ass-kisser is because it's so hard to find *any* guy who treats a woman well that it's painful to let one of these gentlemen go. Unless you'd rather settle on a dude who has all the moxie and competitive fire of France during World War II, it's well worth it to find a man who has opinions and isn't afraid of expressing them.

See, the right guy doesn't think he's right about everything, but even when he does, he respects where you're coming from. He doesn't say yes just because it would be the worst thing in the world to upset you. And he certainly doesn't agree for the sake of agreeing, nor argue for the sake of arguing.

I think we can all agree that Mr. Right has a set of balls and he's not afraid to use them. But when is he using his balls to stand up to you when you're being difficult, and when is he being a stubborn, condescending prick who keeps you in a constant state of apology?

Constructive criticism is when your boyfriend allows you to be you, except when he sees that your behavior is somehow detrimental to *you*. *Destructive* criticism is when your boyfriend tells you to change because he feels that your behavior is detrimental to *him*. Most criticism, it seems, is destructive—and is being given primarily for the sake of the speaker, not the recipient. Psychologists probably call it projection, or enabling, or schizophrenia, for all I know. The point is, you should always ask yourself before giving advice who stands to benefit from it. And you should always question the validity of criticism by considering whether it was intended to help you or to help the critic.

If I ask you to dress more conservatively because it's potentially undermining your chance of a promotion at work, it has nothing to do with me and everything to do with my concern for your well-being. However, if I want you to dress more conservatively because

I'm jealous that other men are looking at you, it has nothing to do with you and everything to do with my own insecurity. Big difference. Last night, I went to a party where all the women present embraced the idea that they not only could change their boyfriends, but *should* change their boyfriends, who, universally, wanted to be changed. And hey, if a guy has poor taste in things and he says, "Here's a credit card, and a key to my apartment; go to town," it's a win/win situation. She gets to transform her pauper into a prince, and he gets an extreme makeover without having to mug for the cameras. But it's pretty difficult to stop tinkering. At one point, Michael Jackson just wanted a smaller nose. Now look what happened.

It takes little more than common sense to refuse to date a domineering man. It takes a lot more to refuse to date a well-meaning weakling of a man. So ask yourself this: Do you respect the guy that you can push around? If a man is so willing to be shaped like a 180-pound sack of Play-Doh, what does that say about him? And what does it say about you, for dating him?

Linda

So you've stopped dating jackasses. Yay! You've stopped being charmed by jealous freaks who won't let you out of the house without your special GPS-enabled underwear. Yay! You've stopped letting guys do that stupid "You're so hard to get to know" flirting thing where they try to get you hot by lecturing you about the content of your dark, conflicted soul, which they know better than you do. Yay! Now, it's full speed ahead, with nothing but people who would never criticize you, who could see you at your most foolish and your most flawed and never, ever say anything about it. Er . . . yay?

You're going to meet a guy, and while you still don't know him all that well yet, he's going to say something to you that's attention grabbing, and new to you, and not complimentary. Something about the way you handled a situation, something about the way you act generally, something about a pattern he sees in your behavior. He won't say it in an attacking way; he'll say it just so you know. And you're not going to be able to stop thinking about it.

The following internal conflict will then emerge: Is this a guy who respects and likes you enough to make an observation to you, the way a friend might, counting on you to be able to handle it and take from it whatever you choose? Or is this a guy who's opening what will become a pattern of lecturing and patronizing, who you will ultimately conclude never actually had any respect for you in the first place? After all, you *want* to wind up with a guy you can ask if you're being crazy and have him look you in the eye and say yes, and have it mean that you're *being* crazy, not that you *are* crazy. That guy is an asset. You'll end up being really glad he was there in time to stop you from sending that letter to your boss with "Dear Clueless Fuckhead" as the salutation.

What you *don't* want is that quasi-big-brother/camp-counselor guy who acts like it's his full-time job to correct your behavior. You don't want a guy who makes you feel like you have to apologize for being yourself, and you don't want a guy whose version of knowing how to talk to you is knowing how to make you feel small.

The first indicator, obviously, is whether he can take the same treatment from you. If he loves to philosophize about the way you treat your parents, but he starts breaking furniture if you say anything about his codependent relationship with his best friend, that's a bad sign. Goose, gander . . . you know the drill.

Another indicator is sheer frequency. If his favorite topic of conversation is your many shortcomings, then that's bad news. Timing is huge, too. People who tell you things because they care about you do it in a way that doesn't humiliate you any more than necessary—they don't do it in front of your friends, or when you're drunk, or when you're already upset about something else. Choosing the least painful moment possible goes a long way toward indicating that he's not just being mean.

People who care about you should expect a lot from you, and it is legitimate to be called out on that basis. It's also possible to be harangued like an errant child until your confidence is shot and every speck of joy has been sucked out of the relationship. Part of telling the good from the bad is differentiating between the people who are trying to fix you and the people who are trying to help you make good choices. Just don't expect it to be easy, because not every expression of love sounds like a love song.

4

The Power of No

The ability to say no in a relationship, in bed, or anywhere else exhibits the kind of confidence that it takes to walk away and be a happy single and, therefore, be happy in a couple. If you establish your worth, you never have to settle for less.

Evan

Remember those old educational films from ninth-grade health class? I do, if only because I'm still afraid of hallucinating about spiders since that's what apparently happens when you smoke pot. The other thing I remember is the concept of peer pressure. "Come on. Try it. It'll make you feel good. All the cool kids are doing it . . ." Seems pretty easy to dismiss because it's really hard to take someone seriously if he's got an orange and brown striped shirt and a Ron Jeremy mustache. Now take away the wardrobe and the facial hair, and focus on the larger message: Someone who you care about, someone who you want to impress, someone who you may even look up to wants you to do something that you don't want to do. Whether we call it by its oft-mocked name or not, peer pressure exists all the time in relationships. And if you don't have that "Just Say No" thing going on, you are quite likely being taken advantage of by your domineering boyfriend.

Him: "You wanna see *The Fast and the Furious* tonight?"
You: (in your head) *No.*
You: (out loud) "Um, sure . . . Whatever you want."

Him: "You ever think about growing your hair long again?"
You: (in your head) *No.*
You: (out loud) "Why? Do you like it better that way?"

Him: "You wanna watch that S&M porn tape with me?"
You: (in your head) *No.*
You: (out loud) "I guess . . . if it turns you on . . ."

Him: "You ever think you'd lose weight if you stopped eating so much?"
You: (in your head) *No, you* dumb motherfucker. *Did you ever think you wouldn't be mistaken for stupid if you stopped speaking so much?*
You: (out loud) "Uhhhhh . . ."

They say that it's the inside that needs fixing more than the outside, but I'm not sure I always agree. The external is really important. If you're unemployed, a job may be the only thing standing between you and happiness. If you have a bad back, the alleviation of pain can drastically alter your mood. If you're in a fight with a friend, making peace may be the only obstacle between you and a good night's sleep. What you can't do is include "boyfriend" on the list of externalities that are the difference between happy you and depressed you.

Women with awesome jobs, great friends, and high self-esteem don't suffer fools gladly. For them, the power of no becomes almost reflexive. If you have a happy and stable life, why settle for Mr. Right Now? A woman who has the capacity to say no is a woman that men want to be with. She's awesome. She's powerful. She commands respect. She's the one we're all fighting over. All because she's willing to walk away.

But many women would rather have someone than no one. Because it's nice to have someone interested. Because she's already invested so much. Because she doesn't want to get back out there and start all over with some other guy who may be worse.

You've probably heard that it's healthy to want, but unhealthy to need. You *want* to fall in love. You don't *need* to fall in love. You need water. You need money. You need shelter. You don't need much else. Needing implies that if you don't have it, you will not be able to survive. I don't know about you, but convincing yourself that a relationship with a man is as essential as breathing is the surest ticket to unhappiness that I can think of.

Linda

If there's one thing that a lot of false starts will teach you, it's that you're on the road to disaster anytime you try to talk yourself out of the way you feel about something.

If you were really going to be able to see *The Fast and the Furious* and not ever think about it again; if you were really going to be able to enjoy the S&M porn tape in spite of your objections; if you were really not going to care one way or another whether you cut your hair . . . well, then it wouldn't matter that much that you say yes when you mean no.

But it doesn't really work that way. Every time you pretend to want something you don't really want, you put a little rock in the pack that you're carrying in the relationship. And if you put enough little rocks in there, it gets so heavy that you can't walk, and all of a sudden, you whip around, look at the guy, and say, "Why the *hell* are you making me carry all these rocks?" And he's thinking, "Rocks? Why are we talking about rocks?"

There's nothing wrong with compromise, but don't do it because you think going along to get along makes you virtuous.

Don't carry weight because you think you have to, or because you want to be crowned the Pain Festival's Martyr Queen, or because you think you'll lose the guy if you ask whether you can put a little bit of it down.

Because really, what *do* you think is going to happen if, when you mean no, you say, well, no? If you think saying no will make him bolt, then not only are you assuming that he wants someone who feels differently about things than you do, which is a problem, but you're also assuming that he's too big of a prick to make any accommodations for the way you feel. If he's going to dump you because you won't go to the Highland Games or the Jessica Simpson concert, then what are you dating him for? For God's sake, how long do you think you can pretend to like Jessica Simpson?

Or is it that you think if you say no, you're going to stare down the fact that it's not a good fit? Maybe it's not that telling him no will make *him* want out, but that it will make *you* want out.

Or do you say yes when you mean no as a way of storing up a point? Not on purpose, though; it's not like you're lying in wait, specifically squirreling away little resentments so that you can spring them on him later in a great and powerful flood. But women in particular get a lot of training in niceness; we're taught that there's something romantic in self-denial, if not downright self-flagellation. The opportunity to walk around with the satisfied feeling that you've given—that you've given and given, because you're a giver!—can be tempting, indeed. It's a little silly, though, because unless the guy you're dealing with is being pushy and demanding, he's not asking you to be a martyr anyway, so you're not doing him any favors. And if he is being pushy and demanding, well . . . you can imagine where that's going.

Not being able to say no doesn't actually make you nice, and it doesn't even make you agreeable. If anything, it probably makes you a little passive-aggressive at some level. Not only that, but it's not especially respectful of the other people in your life to assume that they can't handle any answer from you except blank, grinning agreement. You've got to trust people enough to know that they're not asking you to be a sycophant.

No. Say it to the mirror, say it to the mailman, say it to someone you love. You can do it.

PART III

You're Being a Bitch

You Are What You Hate

Guys Don't Go Both Ways

The Right to Change Your Mind
Should Be Revoked

Don't Play Games

1

You Are What You Hate

Creaky old stereotypes about men who make you crazy are a useful reminder of some of the things you can do to make them crazy as well. Don't answer your cell phone during sex. Don't bolt from commitment. Don't be aloof. You hate that guy. Don't be that guy.

Evan

Not to lend any more credence to the faded phenomenon known as *The Rules,* but did it ever occur to you that the whole hubbub was nothing more than teaching women to act more like men? You ever think that the authors sat around brainstorming the most counterintuitive ways of assisting people to find true love and came up with something like this: "Hmmm . . . if we want women to become objects of desire, they need to take back the power in a relationship . . . so why don't we create a movement that embodies the worst characteristics of men? Yes! That's it. Treat them as poorly as they treat us. It'll work like a charm. Calling when expected? Out. E-mailing if you're thinking of him? Never. Acting on your feelings? Fuhgeddaboutit." As Linda would say, repeat after me: "Two wrongs don't make a right, especially when the two wrongs involve being self-centered and inconsiderate."

You know the stereotypes about men. "He loves his work more than he loves me." "He spends too much time with his friends." "He's totally selfish in bed." "He's emotionally unavailable." No one is defending this type of behavior, but as we push on into the twenty-first century, it's no stretch to say that if equality between the sexes hasn't yet been achieved, we've surely never been closer. With blurry gender roles, it's no surprise that women are taking on some of the more common and less desirable male qualities. The older you get, the more of a life you build for yourself, the less you're gonna want to give it up. It makes perfect sense. It just sucks to date you now because straight men don't really want to date other men. Especially not the selfish ones. So cut it out. Not that full responsibility for compromise falls squarely on your shoulders, but being flexible about the little things is paramount for anyone who is part of a couple.

The workplace archetypes that used to be divided by gender no longer apply. You're just as likely to find a woman doctor on call, a woman with an inseparable posse of friends, or a woman who can't wait to have the guy she slept with just go home already. This is the world that we've created together, in the interest of equality, and I'm all for that. But that leaves men even more confused than we were before (and we have always been, as you know, pretty damn confused), and it leaves women not just feeling like the guy in the relationship, but *being* the guy.

So what does this say about you? It doesn't say that you can't work sixty hours a week. It doesn't say that you can't have girls' night out. It doesn't say you have to call him again after you use him like a cheap sex toy. All it says is that you're truly equal, and with that, you have to be wary of falling into the same traps that your boyfriends do. Abuse your power, and Linda and I will have no choice but to write a "Rules for Men" book. And, boy, will you be sorry.

Linda

We enjoyed the sexual revolution, didn't we? We got better pay, we got the Pill, we got the ability to go to law school and to play professional basketball. I mean, I can't actually *play* basketball, but the patriarchy couldn't stand in my way now, if I were taller, or talented. And sure enough, with the right to do what the boys do, we also got the dangers of . . . well, doing what the boys do.

Okay, pretend you're a really weak-ass dinner-theater comedian, and you're serving ancient clichés along with the flavorless chicken. What are you going to say about men in relationships? Well, you'll say they fear commitment. They work endless hours and don't have time for their partners. They cheat. They don't express affection. Most of these issues have turned green and fuzzy in the back of our collective cultural refrigerator. But when was the last time you considered the possibility that you fear commitment? Or that you're too busy to give a relationship your full attention?

Take the commitment issue, for instance. I don't think fearing commitment is an ethereal, groundless fear that men came up with just because monogamy clashes with their taste for serial dating. It's natural—and appropriate—to like the life you have as a single person and to be nervous about the things you're going to have to give up if you're hooked to somebody else. Women used to be essentially shuttled from their father's house to their husband's with barely a stop in the middle, so what was there for anyone to miss? It seems natural that the more women construct an independent identity for themselves between childhood and marriage, the more they're going to—exactly like a guy—hesitate to give it up. And it's a fair fear to have because your coupled life won't be a replica of your single life with just someone else living in your apartment.

Women don't go to college to catch a husband anymore, either. We go because we have plans, and relationships can disrupt those plans. Commitment means building somebody else into an arc that may stretch from college through years of grad school and internships and whatever other kind of professional purgatory your field requires, and when there's already a lot on your plate, that's a lot to take on, and it makes fear of commitment look not quite so frivolous.

And speaking of work, its demands aren't going to do any favors for your love life, either. In the common romantic imagination, relationships are about an intense connection that exists on a spiritual plane where you can be across the country from each other, hold up a finger like E.T., and feel your chest light up. But you're unlikely to make it work that way indefinitely.

You're ultimately going to have to make room in your life for the things that are important, and if you can't because of other priorities, then that's the choice you're making. However long you hold to that choice, you should embrace it and not feel bad about it. But it's a real choice, the same way it was a choice for Ward Cleaver to decide whether to come home to the family for dinner. And—just as guys started hearing from Phil Donahue or whomever—if you choose your job for a long enough period of time and you choose not to leave room for your personal life, you risk hitting whatever age you find most depressing and discovering that you aren't where you meant to be.

A lot of these issues fall loosely under the umbrella of a form of neglect, I think—a sort of inattention to detail that arises when you expect someone else to do the heavy lifting while you're busy with other parts of your life. Guys get a bad rap (largely undeserved I think) for being unable to pony up emotionally when the rubber hits the road, to the point that women trying to diagnose their failing relationships rarely wonder whether they're guilty of the same behavior.

If you want your relationship to work, you're going to have to show up for it. You're not being graded on a curve, so if you think all you have to do is be a member of the Class of Women that's better at connecting with other people than the Class of Men, it's probably time to get over it. Look at what men do that drives you batty. Look at how they drive you away. We have the vote now, and we own businesses and have jobs and furnish our apartments and don't wait for our weddings to get a stand mixer or a cute set of dishes. None of this means that switching from one stereotypical approach to relationships to another is going to do anyone any favors.

2

Guys Don't Go Both Ways

You want a sensitive man to listen to you and share his feelings with you? You want a strong man who never shows a chink in his armor? Realize that these are different people and stop expecting your boyfriend to fulfill your every emotional need.

Evan

You may have heard that men want their girlfriends to be like mothers in the kitchen and whores in the bedroom. There's much more to winning a man's heart, of course, but for simplicity's (and broad stereotype's) sake: great food + great sex = happy man. Throw in a pair of season tickets to his favorite team and you may just get him to sign your marriage license in blood. I've heard some women complain about this paradigm, which some see as an impossible standard. "So he wants me to wait on him, hand and foot, and then be his own personal love slave after I'm done with the dishes?" Yeah, something like that. But since it's not all that realistic, we accept and appreciate the occasional batch of cookies or some weekend morning lovemaking. Relationships are about compromise, y'know?

It's a tall order to make like Julia Child and Jenna Jameson all at once. We don't deny this, which is why you've probably never had a guy request it before. The male parallel for this, as you may have discerned from the chapter heading, is when you're asking him to be your "got-it-all-under-control" father and your "we-really-need-to-talk" best friend simultaneously.

So here's the deal: There are plenty of strong men who can shed a tear. There are plenty of emotional ones who won't collapse under the weight of your personal turmoil. But the balance is rarely 50/50—more like 60/40—which means that, in almost all circumstances, your boyfriend is going to be lacking in some capacity. Sucks, doesn't it?

Yes, men can change, and do change, as they see fit, as time goes by. However, for the most part, if we're in our thirties, we're pretty much the same guys we're going to be in another five years. Getting angry at a man for staying constant is like getting angry at the sky for staying blue. The Rock is not going to always remember to ask about your day when you come home from work, and The Artist is not always going to have the strength to keep it all to himself if he hasn't sold any sculptures. If you are dating The Rock, appreciate him for the emotionless pillar that he is. If that's not good enough because you feel safe but you don't feel connected, that's fine. Find yourself a new guy who talks to you. If you want a communicator, accept that when a man opens up, it isn't always just going to be about listening to your feelings but sharing some of his as well. Men revealing their feelings makes them vulnerable, just as it does for women. And the last thing any guy wants is to have the feelings that he's been encouraged to share held against him.

More of my friends fit the bill of the traditional, noncommunicative male—and often find that their efforts fall short when dealing with their girlfriends. These guys come from families in which men were men: bringing home the bacon, eating someone else's cooking, maybe even smoking a pipe and chopping wood. Attempting to turn one of these guys into your closest confidante is like trying to turn your closest confidante into one of these guys—in other words, it's a big, honking waste of time.

You've heard it before, but I'll say it again: Love him or leave him. Because no man can be all things at all times, no matter how bad you want him to be.

Linda

One of my favorite people—who happens to be a man—told me once that every guy secretly believes the song "Desperado" was written about him. And while that may not be strictly true, I do suspect that just as an awful lot of women feel whipsawed between the expectation that they be assertive and the expectation that they be nice, an awful lot of men feel that lonely-cowboy business fairly acutely. They feel that pull to show strength while hinting at unseen vulnerability.

Not for nothing, either. Confessional flashes from men can be just as sexy as they're reputed to be, or men wouldn't have been using them for the last, like, *five hundred years* to pick up chicks.

On the other hand, I'm not going to lie to you: I have my moments when I instinctively gravitate toward old-fashioned stoicism. There are times when I don't care about being listened to, I don't want to explain how I'm feeling, and I'm really just looking for the shoulder that won't collapse. And there are times when I'm charmed by having some guy stick his nose in my business and offer to fight my battles. It's an understandable instinct to think that in a crisis, you could do worse than a bloodless crusader type who'll stand in front of you like a bouncer as the complications of your life stagger up to you like smelly drunks.

Unfortunately, guys who look like stoics are usually that way because they've trained themselves to be a little bit tone-deaf emotionally—to tolerate shifting currents without reacting. But that guy may not be good at reading you. Why? Exactly because he's emotionally tone-deaf. It's how he survives. It's not that he secretly wants to talk about his feelings and he's afraid to; he really doesn't want to. And he really doesn't want to hear about yours, either, because he has no idea what to say to you.

The point is that, as Evan says, the guy who's like a rock is not going to turn into a feather pillow, nor is he going to be able to do a decent approximation of a feather pillow just because it suits you in the particular moment. If you're going to embrace the steadfastness that Rock Man offers, you may have to go elsewhere for your heavy-duty one-on-one personal confessionals.

The flip side? If you're going to pick a guy because he's emotionally aware, then you can't be angry when it means life is more complicated. You especially can't make it seem like he's weaker for it. Stoicism isn't a sign of strength, anyway; it's a chosen approach to the same crap everyone else is dealing with. If you want comfort in the form of somebody who will listen to you and care about your problems and absorb a little of your stress, be willing to offer the same thing without complaining. Find somebody who works at the same emotional pitch you do, and don't expect to crank the volume up and down at will.

3

The Right to Change Your Mind Should Be Revoked

Don't demand the right to set arbitrary rules, let alone change them every five minutes. Act like a crazy person and you'll be treated like one.

Evan

Imagine you have a fickle boss at work. Monday, he tells you he likes black uni-ball pens. Tuesday, he tells you that he prefers blue ones. Wednesday, he asks you to rewrite all his notes in green. Thursday, he wonders why he even keeps notes at all and asks you to shred them. Friday, you are told to type the shredded notes into a Word document.

Imagine that you're our fickle boss. Now imagine how difficult it can be to keep up with you.

You may never have actually uttered aloud, "A woman has the right to change her mind," but you certainly have heard it. When spoken, it's usually with a coy smirk—the underlying sentiment being, "Yes, I'm altering my decision, but, come on . . . you know you still love me anyway." If this image doesn't resonate, try to re-call that look you give a cop when he pulls you over for speeding. You smile and bat your eyes at him and, after a moment, he lets you go. Really, what choice does he have? You're adorable. He's a guy. Everybody wins.

Changing your mind is a choice, not a personality trait. Every-one has the capacity to be somewhat consistent; some relinquish consistency when it suits their purposes.

When Linda and I allude to changing your mind, we're not talking about the reasonable kind of switch that comes with gathering and processing new information. If you hear on the radio that there's traffic on the freeway, choosing the side streets on the fly makes perfect sense. If you discover that he's cheating on you, you have every right to reconsider that relationship's viability. It's more when the rules change with no warning that your partner may find himself struggling a bit.

Once upon a time, I had a girlfriend who gave me a lesbian porn tape that she owned because she thought I'd enjoy it. What made her gift particularly perplexing was that she later barked at me for reading a *Playboy* magazine because it exemplified the ways in which men objectify women. Now I'm not saying she didn't have a rationale—something about porn being for both genders while *Playboy* is strictly for the male gaze—but you have to be somewhat of a logician to parse the two. Essentially, I was being vilified for partaking in a less hard-core but more insidious form of pornography, albeit one about which I couldn't possibly care less. My failure to grasp the nuance of her viewpoint was the source of great agita, to the point that I finally asked her for written guidelines to inform me which porn was acceptable to her. Whether you agree with her or agree with me about porn isn't the point of the story—the point is that my inability to find some internal consistency in her viewpoint left me forever walking on eggshells around her. That's no way to be with your best friend.

If you've ever had a guy who ran hot and cold with you, then you know what I mean. He tells you he loves you, then he doesn't call you for a week. He says you're the only one but is always hanging out with his ex-girlfriend. He's faithful as a Labrador yet treats you like a mutt. What do you do with a guy like that? You love him, you hate him, and all you want to know is where you stand with him.

In a world where people make up the rules as they go along, it's impossible for a well-meaning guy to ever know where he stands. This may be a familiar dance to us, but it's not a fun one. If you're making up your dance steps as you go along, you can't bitch at us when we step on your feet.

Linda

Stereotypes about women are a funny thing. The way they box you in can make your head pound with frustration.

But being boxed in has its insidious advantages. What you aren't capable of, after all, you aren't expected to do. Convince people that you can't cook, and they're not going to be surprised when they come to your house and you serve frozen lasagna. Claiming weaknesses you don't have sounds preposterous, but it's a genuine temptation—kind of like selling your soul to the devil. When you stare down the barrel of one of those really strange moments where you can't explain why you're acting the way you are, it's remarkable how easy it is to fall back on exactly what Evan's talking about. It's easier to accept a stale cliché suggesting that you aren't *supposed* to make sense than it is to figure out where your internal logic has gone wonky.

I don't know a lot of women who will explicitly pull out the line, "Well, you know, it's a woman's right to change her mind." Nor do I know a lot of women who do it intentionally, or with any kind of malice. I do, however, know women who do it by implication. How? By acting like their bullshit is adorable. Like their mercurial irrationality is endearing, because ho-ho-ho, chicks are crazy!

You can't let this happen. Under emotional pressure you'll feel how simple it would be to cover it all with a giant load of cute. Cute is easy. Cute is just a smile and a little false indignation, and it's over before you know it. And the only thing you've given up is the right to be taken seriously.

You can't have it both ways. You can choose to change the rules at will, to react with nut-ball jealousy, and to otherwise wrap yourself up in every bad stand-up comedy routine that's ever started with, "The thing about my wife is . . ." You can do that, and a surprising number of women do. There are two problems, though.

The first problem is fairly obvious: It's unfair to the guy you're with. There's nothing joyfully madcap about dealing with people who don't make any sense, as you know if you've ever experienced it.

But second, and more important: You can't expect to turn it off. Once you portray yourself as divorced from logic, you're never going to have another serious conversation from a position of strength. You'll be in the middle of making a perfectly fair and reasonable argument, and you'll see it on the guy's face—a little smirk. And you'll realize that you have handed him the reason not to listen to you. You've already traded respect for freedom from constraint, and you can't trade it back.

If you're old enough for a relationship that's serious, then you're old enough to expect yourself to make sense and to allow other people to expect the same of you. Take Evan's story about the lesbian porn tape. There are possible explanations for what was really going on there, which was certainly not that women are genetically programmed to arbitrarily change rules. Suppose, for instance, that a woman was trapped between wanting to seem sexually adventurous in situations that she can control and feeling threatened by the possibility that a guy who seeks out naked chicks on his own isn't happy with her. Maybe that's true; maybe it's not. But if you found yourself in that circumstance and were to acknowledge that conflict and talk about it, you might get somewhere. But if you smother it by making up bizarre, multiple-footnote explanations of why the obviously absurd is, in fact, patently logical, you're going to wind up in a fight about categories of porn, which has nothing to do with what's going on at all.

Beyond college at the latest, no one you should bother with thinks that being crazy is cute. They may tolerate it, they may overlook it, they may try to help you outgrow it, but it does not endear you to them. It's like people who regularly get insanely drunk to the point where you have to carry them out of bars. After a certain age, that's a huge drag, and seeing someone do it on the assumption that other people think it's hilarious has a certain air of pathos. Women who act nutty in that shrill, conspicuous way are giving off the same vibe, whether they know it or not.

You're not a stereotype, and you're not a fool, and you're not a helpless cream puff. You don't need to be humored and handheld like you're taking a remedial class in reason. You're an adult woman, and we're a perfectly logical species. Step up.

4

Don't Play Games

Women, in assuming that men always play games, trip them-selves up when the guys are actually trying to be straightfor-ward. Let's just all stop this cycle of absurdity and love each other, shall we?

Evan

I don't know a single woman who says that she likes games. I don't know a single man who says he likes games. So if nobody likes games, why does everyone play them? Ask women and they'll say they play them because they think that men do. Ask men and they'll say they play them because they think women do. Talk about a vicious circle. Not only is nobody being real, but who has time to make any true connections, what with all the aloofness, posturing, and calculating?

Correct me if I'm wrong, but isn't the point of a relationship to be loved for who you are? Isn't the ideal partner a nonjudgmental one, who lets you be yourself without holding your flaws against you? And if, in fact, this is the case, why do women spend so much time putting on a front to get some game-playing schmuck to chase them? Is it because if he chases you, it means that he's inter-ested? Let me tell you something: Any guy who chases you is not doing it for *you*; he's doing it for the chase. Like a cat following a flashlight on a wall, or a greyhound racing after a mechanical rab-bit, it's largely involuntary and instinctive. Plus, it just puts off the process of letting him get to know you for who you really are, un-less you plan to revel in your coy charade for the next forty years.

I've got no doubt that there are a number of women who played by *The Rules* and connived their way into a man's heart. Kudos to them. I'd also bet the farm that just as many men have written off women after a few days of unreturned calls. I know I have. The Rules Girls might justify their behavior by saying that the right guy would have followed up—because if he liked her enough, he'd put up with her bullshit. Yeah, good luck with that.

There is this perception that men are just dying to jump through hoops for you. It's not true. The fewer hoops, the better. The only thing we don't want is someone who is so desperate to mate that she loses all self-respect. But if a guy likes a girl, and he lets her know in no uncertain terms, the best thing she can do is reciprocate, without hesitation. Case in point: I've got an e-mail in my in-box from a woman who took two weeks to write back to my last e-mail. You think I'm going to respond to her immediately? Hell, no. Am I playing games? Hell, yeah. Would I play them if she replied to me in a timely fashion? C'mon . . . what do you think?

The thing about games is that they create obstacles where there are none. It's like putting a tall fence around your apartment and challenging the guy to figure out a way inside, when you could simply let him in the front door. Assuming the guy has other options, why wouldn't he go to a less treacherous home instead of trying to scale your wall? Sure, you might find the guy who climbed Everest "because it was there," but is he the guy you want to date? If so, congratulations to you incredibly challenging folks. I'm sure your mastery of being detached will come in real handy a few years down the road when one of you loses a job or a parent.

A close friend of mine told me that she asked out a guy with whom she had a great first date. She had two tickets to see Cher and wanted him to join her. He thanked her but said he wasn't a Cher fan. Instead, he asked for a rain check and suggested that they maybe catch another concert. My friend took this to mean that he wasn't interested in her. I reminded her that they weren't a couple and had only gone out once. Why should he go on a date that he didn't want to be on?

My friend held her ground. Despite the fact that he was not rejecting her but, rather, was rejecting Cher, she still thought it was clear that he wasn't interested. Her feelings were backed up by the fact that he never called her again. Then again, if a woman I barely knew gave me a hard time about not wanting to spend three hours watching a fifty-something pop star shake her tail feathers, I'd probably be out the door too.

Linda

There's no getting around the fact that some people play games. They have head-fakes and spin moves, and they feint left and go right until it makes you dizzy. You can compare it to poker, you can compare it to football, you can compare it to whatever you like—the bottom line is that you will, at times, run into guys who are all strategy. Every act of apparent sincerity has an equal and opposite ulterior motive, and if on a particular day half of what they tell you is true, they are batting ahead of their average. These people exist—men, women, high school students, senior citizens . . . I've met some very manipulative babies and dogs, come to think of it. And at least once in your life, you're not going to see it coming until it's too late. That is, to say the least, the bad news.

The good news is that not everyone is like that. Sure, there's strategy inherent in perfectly innocent flirtation and so forth; life would be bland without it. But once you get past that, it's possible to find people are relatively straight shooters—they ask for what they want, they generally try to tell you the truth, and most of their mistakes are sins of foolishness, not malice. You're probably trying to be one of these people.

But if you're used to games, it can be really difficult not to spar on instinct. Everybody's potentially up to something, right? You might as well hedge your bets and do a little maneuvering *just in case* that's what he's doing, right? Besides, asking for what you want is hard, while making people guess at what you want is pretty easy. Send in a hissy fit that looks a lot like anger when what you're really feeling is hurt—well, hell, he'll know what that means, right? Act like you don't care when really you do—don't they always say men like a challenge? They like it when you pretend not to care if they call you, right? And they like it if you act standoffish and rude because then they can chase you, which they find enticing, right?

Right. There *is* a kind of guy who likes that crap, and it's the same kind of guy who's going to play games with *you*. Just as having red hair is a good way to attract men who like red hair, playing games is a great way to attract men who like games.

What you really *don't* want to do is screw around with a decent guy who's trying to be straight with you. They hate it, and rightly so. Suppose a situation comes up that might be nothing but might be something more sinister—a single canceled date, for instance. Now, certainly, that could be a bad sign. He might have gotten a better offer. He might be trying to make you crazy. He might be starting a bizarre mind-fuck in which he's going to cancel every fourth date in order to keep you from ever getting comfortable. He might not be into you! If you imagine that he's doing any of those things, you could try refusing to take his phone calls for a while, because he might be fascinated by the challenge. You could arrange to go out with someone else and make sure he sees you. You could say something to one of his friends and wait for it to get back to him. You could cry! At least he'd never be able to say he got the better of you.

But suppose it's none of those things. Suppose he badly wanted to go but work legitimately interfered—just like he told you it did—and he's looking forward to rescheduling. If you respond to this guy with any of the nonsense from the last paragraph, he's probably going to leave. And can you blame him?

There comes a point at which ridiculous behavior apparently inspired by machinations you learned at the prom has *no chance* of benefiting you. It can attract *only* men who are bad news, and it will alienate *all* men who are good news. Its only conceivable advantage is that it does leave you slightly less exposed because trying to mess with other people's heads will give you a certain illusion of control. Trust me, it's not worth it.

If you think the guy is screwing with your head, *drop him*. If you don't think he's screwing with your head, don't screw with his. It's not nice, it makes people angry, and—not for nothing—it's exhausting. Not to go all *WarGames* on you, but it's really true that the only way to win is not to play.

PART IV

You Know How to Be the *Girl Friend*, but Not the *Girlfriend*

Use Honesty to Manipulate

———

Jealousy? Ha!

———

Humpty Dumpty Did *Not* Live
Happily Ever After

1

Use Honesty to Manipulate

The easiest way to get what you want is, surprisingly, to tell the truth. That is, "good truth," not "bad truth." Being honest for the sake of being honest can be very dangerous. See Liar Liar *and you'll understand.*

Evan

Okay everybody, get out your pencils for Lesson 1: Good Truth vs. Bad Truth.

Since in real life there are no definitive answers, I won't tell you my opinions on the below statements. I'll merely submit these examples for your consideration, and you can determine for yourself whether it's useful to say whatever may be on your mind.

- Saying "I think you need a more financially stable job" to a guy who's satisfied with his less-than-lucrative career.
- Saying "You can be very callous/selfish/argumentative/ insecure/annoying" to a guy you've only gone out with once.
- Saying "Why do you get so defensive when I offer my unsolicited negative opinions of you? I'm just being honest."

Ah, you gotta love honesty.

Please realize that bad truth doesn't negate the fact that your point might be 100 percent correct. Understanding bad truth simply acknowledges that there's a time and place for everything. And in a society that encourages people to get in touch with their feelings and speak their minds, sometimes the filter between good truth and bad truth gets lost. When offenders are pressed on the concept of bad truth, they tend to wrap themselves in the blanket of honesty, like Olympians wrapping themselves in the American flag. "What do you want me to do? Stifle my opinions? Do you want me to lie to you?" Um, yeah, sometimes we do.

The best anecdote I can recall to illustrate good truth came when I was in my late twenties. A beautiful woman had written to me on Match.com. We talked for a week before meeting, went on a spectacular date, and ended up at my place. The next morning, she made it clear that she wasn't looking for a boyfriend. She'd been in monogamous relationships for the greater part of ten years and was just hoping to date around for a while. She even confessed to me that she was seeing about five other guys. This may not have been good news, but it was certainly good *truth*—laying it all out on the table with the express intent of not hurting me.

Undaunted, I mustered up the confidence to offer her some good truth, namely, that I really liked her and wanted to see her regularly. But since I couldn't twist her arm, all I could do was accept her situation and roll with it. With one caveat. I made her promise me that if she was out with another guy and found herself thinking of me, that'd be the last time she'd see him. After all, why go out with someone else when I'm at home waiting for her? The cocky gesture was a calculated risk: She could have laughed at me, could have dumped me, could have kept me as Boy Toy #5. But she didn't. In fact, she did exactly what I'd hoped and became my girlfriend a few weeks later. I got what I wanted just by accepting her for who she was and stating my purest intentions. I liked her. I wanted to date her exclusively. I told her so and demanded nothing unreasonable. If this ploy had backfired and she told me to take a hike, *c'est la vie*. No harm done—to either of us.

Think of the times when someone has told you something you didn't want to hear, but they were doing it for the right reasons. Like when one girlfriend told me to keep my emotions in check when negotiating a contract. Or another who chastened me for being insensitive to a friend of hers when I was oblivious to my own behavior. Good truth, therefore, can dovetail with constructive criticism. Both parties can feel positive about the exchange because it's real and it's for the greater good of all involved. Ultimately, your partner may not always react the way you wanted, but at least it won't be because you did anything wrong or were anything less than true to yourself.

Linda

Being against lying is like being against disco. In theory, everybody will tell you they're with you, but in practice, it's a lot more complicated than that. And when it's necessary, definitions will be bent beyond recognition to accommodate situations about which we can all agree. Even the most hard-core disco hater will tell you that for her purposes, "Everlasting Love" is not disco, even though it is. Similarly, even the most hard-core devotee of honesty will tell you that, for her purposes, saying "I would have never noticed that [pimple/mismatched outfit/social faux pas] if you hadn't told me" isn't lying, even though it is.

We can all probably agree that telling the truth for its own sake isn't always a great idea. Therefore, I highly recommend deceiving people as often as possible, because it will save you a lot of hassle and unpleasant conflict. *Vaya con Dios!* The end!

No? Okay, no. Look, the truth has a lot of potential downsides. If you decide to be straight with people, you're going to limit your options. There's only one answer to how you really feel or what you really want. If it's ugly, it's ugly. If it's inconvenient, surprising, expensive, or depressing, you're stuck with that. Furthermore, lies aren't really from you, so they aren't really pieces of you, so if they don't go over well, who cares, right? Who cares if a carefully crafted routine elicits nothing but a big eye-roll? You can always come up with something else. If you're genuinely revealing your heart, of course, you can't switch it out for the next available alternative quite so easily.

You already know plenty of reasons it's better not to lie to people, because they're the same reasons you don't like when people lie to you. People make choices and develop feelings based on what you're telling them, and giving them bad information isn't entirely fair. If you end a relationship because the guy is boring, irritating, and bad in bed, but what you tell him is that you "need time to think," you're inviting him to linger like the last drunk friend at a dull party—unwelcome and unaware that he's supposed to go away, for real. I'm not suggesting you tell him he's boring, irritating, and bad in bed, but I am suggesting you tell him it's over. You know you're not planning on giving anything more to the relationship; chaining him to your doorstep out of politeness doesn't do him any favors.

Building relationships on false foundations can also be very isolating for you. You have to remember what impression you're trying to create, and then you have to apply that filter to everything you think and feel. If you're telling the truth, then with appropriate adjustments for basic courtesy, you can rediscover the art of speaking extemporaneously. And you, acting on instinct? You, following your glorious hippie bliss, speaking your mind? That's who you really are, and your relationships are going to mean a lot more to you when the love you're getting is being offered to someone who's actually *you*.

Straightforwardness is also an excellent way of getting what you really want. If you're in a relationship with someone who cares about you (which you'd better be), then he's going to try to make you happy and give you the things that you need for that to happen. Being shy about the way you feel is a tragic waste of all that willingness to make an effort on your behalf.

On the other hand, I'm not advocating compulsive confessionalizing. This isn't a reality show; you don't have to sit down with an unseen interviewer and pour out your innermost thoughts about everything that's ever happened. There are times to keep your mouth shut, and there are times to shade unimportant truths to avoid doing unnecessary damage. What's important is making sure that the person who winds up in your relationships is the person you actually are. Besides, the truth is a powerful thing. Quite possibly more powerful than disco.

2

Jealousy? Ha!

You should never have to raise your voice or check up on your boyfriend's whereabouts. If you can't trust him, something is very, very wrong.

Evan

I've never cheated, but I've been cheated on. In fact, I may have been cheated on more than once, but I can't really know that anymore than I know whether someone faked an orgasm, can I?

I bring up my own track record not because it's sterling, but because a lot of women use their history as an excuse for their jealous attitude. "I've had guys cheat on me before, and I swore I'd never go out with another cheater again," many women will say. Which is a reasonable stance, except for one small thing: You can't control him when he's not there. He can do whatever he wants. If you're under the illusion that any amount of jealousy is going to straighten him out, I hate to break it to you, but you're wrong. If the death penalty doesn't deter felons, keeping a hawk's eye on your man isn't going to stop him from screwing around.

Therein lies the futility of jealousy. It accomplishes absolutely nothing except letting your partner know that despite the implications of trust that come with a committed relationship, you don't trust him. Then, of course, there are the accompanying arguments that come with you listening to his phone calls, reading his e-mails, and interrupting his cocktail party conversations with female friends.

I've heard women defend jealousy—not in themselves, but in their own boyfriends. Something to the effect of: "At least I know he cares about me." As if a guy who forbids you from talking to your ex-boyfriend is a paragon of kindness. Regardless of your gender, you don't have to be all that observant to see that jealousy is not flattering to either party in a couple. Instead, it's a totally useless emotion that reflects your level of security more than it reflects on someone's propensity to cheat.

My first love was a woman who got upset whether I was conversing with a seventeen-year-old checkout girl or a fifty-year-old bartender with two college-age daughters. Am I friendly? Yes. Am I flirty? Sure. Am I trying to get in on my drink server's sweet Medicare coverage? Not quite.

Some nights, it's fun to be the inseparable couple, locked arm in arm, making the rounds with witty bon mots and urbane conversation. Then there are nights when it's fun to go your separate ways. Let's face it, in the scope of a long-term relationship, an evening of not feeling bound to your partner can be liberating. Being able to talk to whomever you want without repercussion can be exciting. And knowing that, after all the small talk, you'd *still* choose to go home with the same person is positively life-affirming.

While folks should be more mindful and considerate of a sensitive (read: jealous) partner, you can't stop flirts from flirting anymore than you can stop smokers from smoking, joggers from jogging, or tall people from blocking your view at concerts. If you don't like it, that's fine, but chances are it's not going to change. Habits change, personality traits don't.

I know you've considered this before, but if you're concerned that your boyfriend is a risk to cheat, maybe you shouldn't be dating him. I mean, you can pull a Hillary and ignore it. Or you could pull an Uma and dump his ass. But you're not going to make an honest man out of a dishonest man. If anything, your jealousy will drive him in the other direction.

Oh, and if you're reading this and cursing under your breath because the only reason you're so jealous is that the bastard *is* a cheater, take a deep breath and redirect that anger at him. I'm not telling you to date a cheater; I'm telling you to trust him or leave him. And yes, it is that simple.

Linda

I have this theory of porn and waitresses. But let me come back to that.

It may be because I have a touch of the flirt bug myself (both because I initiate it and especially because I am beyond helpless to resist it), but this is one area where I have what tends to be a more stereotypically guylike viewpoint, which is that I cannot understand for the life of me why flirting is so contentious.

Sure, if we're talking about a guy who will take you to a party and spend the entire evening with some other woman sitting on his lap, that's bad. That's disrespectful to you, and it's a "what are you going to do about it?" brand of aggression. Ditto excessive flirting with anyone who has actually made herself available to sleep with him (bad, bad), particularly including exes (bad, bad, bad), or any woman who evidently doesn't respect you and what your position is. You have the right, in short, not to have a guy try to show you up, impress his friends with how nonwhipped he is, remind you constantly how many options he has, or feed his ego a steady diet of women he could have.

But what about run-of-the-mill friendly flirting, particularly when you're sitting right there? That has nothing to do with you. Like it or don't like it on its own merits, but don't take it personally, because it probably isn't personal. Men who flirt? They're flirts. They'll flirt when they're out with family, out with friends, out with a woman, or out alone. They will flirt with plants, pets, food, and furniture. Forget *America's Next Top Model*, they'll flirt at a party celebrating the opening of the Westminster Dog Show. I'm telling you, that one is a character trait. Provided you have no other reason to believe he doesn't know where the line is, don't start a fight about it.

It's exactly like porn. If you don't dig it when your boyfriend looks at porn because you think that porn is distasteful and degrading to women and contributes to an underground drug economy you read about in *Ms.* and now you feel really, really strongly about it, that's fine. Object to the *Sports Illustrated* swimsuit issue on principle? Go with that. There are vegetarian guys driving hybrid cars all over the country who totally agree with you; find yourself one of them and live a long and happy life with no magazines in the house except *Mother Jones*. No point in driving yourself crazy.

And what about guys who are porn *addicts*? Guys who can't relate to women not dressed in straps and buckles, guys who are spending so much time jacking off to high-heel-wearing, bug-stomping vixens of streaming video that they are no longer interested in sex with you? *That* is a problem. And obviously if it is not just pedestrian porn, but porn that involves the young, the blood relatives, the barnyard animals . . . yeah, set your boundaries. But if you have talked yourself into the idea that a guy who really loves you will cease to be aroused by porn, you are living in a tragically erotica-deprived fool's paradise. Go buy a copy of *Scruples* or something else by Judith Krantz and . . . read until you get over it.

Thus, my theory of porn and waitresses. If your boyfriend wouldn't pick you for a *relationship* over the barmaid or the girl being licked by the gardener while her best friend looks on and the chicka-wocka music plays, or if he'd give up his relationship with you to indulge in either of those things, then that's where your problem lies. But flirting with the checkout girl isn't choosing her over you, and getting off on the gardener's friend? That's not a rejection of you. That's sort of how people are.

Besides, getting into arguments about whether the flirting you

know about presents a threat of unfaithfulness seems a little pointless anyway. A guy who's otherwise going to cheat on you isn't going to *not* cheat on you because you get pinchy and paranoid about
it—after all, if he's going to cheat on you in the first place, he really doesn't care how you feel about it. He's not doing it because
he thinks you won't mind. A guy who's *not* going to cheat on you
is only going to get pissed off that you don't trust him. You stand
to gain nothing.

It's exactly like Evan said: Trust the guy or don't. If you honestly believe you're being cheated on, then of course, confront
him—for the sake of your health, if for no other reason. But if
you're acting on the simple assumption that a person who really
loves you should never again see either the flirtatious or naked appeal of anyone but you, then you're basically committing yourself
to waiting around for somebody who's going to lie his ass off,
because that just isn't the way it works.

3

Humpty Dumpty Did *Not* Live Happily Ever After

Why? Because he broke into so many pieces, there was no way to put him back together. Confront issues as they come, because if you don't, they can build up and destroy the foundation of the relationship irreparably.

Evan

You know how couples break up and get back together about three times before they ever officially call it quits? It looks a little silly and futile from the outside, but it makes perfect sense when you're in the middle of it. I mean, you're best friends, you've invested everything in each other, and the last thing you want to do is give up, only to meet a bunch of strangers who probably won't come close to measuring up to your current partner. Most of the time, if one party is willing to give up the relationship, it's doomed, but sometimes couples can be saved with a little therapy, effort, or sacrifice. Occasionally, when the onus is on one party to change or risk losing everything, he/she will voluntarily change. At that point, even if things fall apart, you're both left with the comfort of knowing that you gave it everything you had. The relationship took work, you put in the work, and if that means you're breaking up, at least you have no regrets.

I have plenty of regrets about my last relationship.

Well aware that I'm not big on unnecessary criticism, my girlfriend dumped me abruptly, right before we were supposed to take a roadtrip to Vegas. For the life of me, I didn't see it coming.

We hadn't been at our happiest, but I didn't think we were at any critical juncture in our relationship. If anything, I figured that the fact that I scored tickets to see Cirque du Soleil might set us on the right path. Not quite. She'd had enough. She was thinking about it for a month but never brought it up. Just dropped the bomb and left me to deal with the fallout.

There are a million reasons that she broke up with me. Okay, maybe like, four or five. But they're entirely valid, and I'm glad she was honest with me after we split. Still, it sure would have been nice to have a clue that her discontent was so deep-seated. Maybe there were things I could have done to explain myself, or understand her needs better, or, yes, even *change* in order to accommodate her. I didn't even get a chance. All I got was an exit interview evaluating the previous quarter's performance as I was shown the door.

In the aftermath, I learned that we viewed our relationship very differently. What appeared to be the easiest, drama-free relationship I'd ever had was, to her, way too turbulent. Well, of course, it was. She was a merry-go-round, placidly going around in circles. I was more of a roller coaster, filled with ups and downs. She came from a family that didn't fight. I learned growing up that all opinions should be expressed freely. Successful relationships are all about finding the balance. The way I see it, unless you're dating someone very boring who has no opinions or very weak who doesn't have the courage to express her opinions, there's going to be some turbulence. There can't *not* be turbulence when your lives merge and suddenly you have to account for another person's tastes, feelings, and sensitivities.

The big question, therefore, is not whether there'll be conflict— oh, there will be—but, rather, how you handle the conflict as it arises. Do you let it go gracefully, or do you carry around a grudge? They say "choose your battles," but over the course of a lifetime, all those battles are tantamount to a full-fledged war. How can you minimize the strenuous effects of "She spends too

much money" or "He doesn't listen when I speak"? It's not by
sweeping those things under the rug, that's for sure. Because one
day that rug is going to be so puffy and jagged that you'll never be
able to walk on it. Such are the latent effects of not dealing with
issues as they come up.

I hate to return to the porn thing, but a friend of mine was once
shocked—*shocked*, I tell you—when, in the process of helping her
boyfriend move, she inadvertently discovered his large porn stash in
the closet (not to be confused with large porn 'stache, which is actually legitimate grounds for dismissal). Evidently, she wasn't privy to
Linda's theory of porn and waitresses, because this discovery really
bothered her. He defused the situation by telling her that the porn
wasn't his, that he was actually "holding it for a friend." (Pause for
laughter.) Despite her sensitivities, she accepted this explanation,
not wanting to rock the boat. Well, guess what? Later, when they'd
moved in together, she realized that this porn thing wasn't a tiny
fetish at all. Turns out he was running up large phone sex charges on
her bill from the living room, all while she was asleep in their bedroom. Surprisingly, the two star-crossed lovers didn't make it. Sigh.

So what do we learn from this sordid little tale, besides the fact
that phone sex is expensive? Mostly, it illustrates that just because
you ignore a problem doesn't mean it goes away. Instead, it's far
more likely to fester and branch out into other undesirable incar-
nations. I'm not saying you should nitpick—that would go against
everything we've said thus far in the book. I am saying that if you
have a problem with your partner that you just can't ignore, deal
with it the way you'd like to be dealt with if someone had a problem with you. It probably doesn't involve screaming or finger-
pointing or name-calling or any of the other histrionics that
accompany most arguments. Facing a problem head-on as it arises
not only gives you the best chance to overcome it as a couple, but
makes it more likely not to surface in a more dangerous fashion a
few years later—when you're both in a whole lot deeper.

Linda

Have you ever heard the urban legend about how if you swallow gum, it stays in your stomach forever? It's a gruesomely fascinating idea, that you will gradually accumulate a giant wad of gum somewhere in your digestive system, one comprising all the Big Red, all the Juicy Fruit, all the Bubble Yum, and all the Bazooka of your life. It would grow from the size of a golf ball to the size of a baseball to the size of a soccer ball, just sort of sitting idle until you get rid of it, like one of those crazy-ass benign tumors they take out on the Discovery Channel at three in the morning. Unfortunately, this wonderful idea turns out to be entirely false. You digest a little gum, and the rest just sort of passes on through.

Why am I telling you this? Because there are times when it's safe to shut up and not bother making a federal case out of everything—in other words, just swallow the gum. If it's going to behave like gum behaves in *reality*, by eventually taking care of itself, you're fine. But if it's going to behave like gum behaves in the *legend*, building up in an ever-expanding mass, then you really shouldn't swallow it, and you're better off spitting it out, even if it's messy. See what I mean?

Be assured that I couldn't be more serious about this particular tortured metaphor. If whatever you're angry about is going to sit there undigested for decades to come, you're not only going to be perpetually annoyed by it, but you're also going to bring it up in vague ways from time to time, whether you mean to or not, because it's still there. Just keeping you company, biding its time. Growing and growing, one resentful little stick at a time. That's bad.

It's not easy to confront problems. It's tempting to look at friction as a disheartening failure, as if the perfection of your relationship is measured on a scale of 100 points, with a point subtracted for every time you get in a fight. This isn't limited to your romantic life, either; people are this way, about friends, about family, and about people they work with. If you take that attitude, that fighting is failing, then the perfectionist in you is likely to avoid it as much as possible.

Fighting is also scary, particularly with people with whom you aren't yet well connected. One of the great things about good relationships is that you feel like you can put weight on them without being afraid they're going to collapse under you, and when you fight, you're on rickety legs all of a sudden. Uncertainty is disorienting and tiring, and every time you feel your voice rising, you're less sure than you were a minute ago that you still like him and he still likes you, even if it's at that primitive level where you'd know not to worry if you could step out of the situation and think—which, of course, you can't, because your head is doing ninety and your mouth may still be ahead of it.

People wind up choking down a lot of discontentment instead of saying anything when they're unhappy. They grind their teeth down to little nubs trying to keep the peace. It's an understandable impulse, but just remember, conflict is ugly and unpleasant, but it beats having a ball of Bubblicious removed from your abdomen between late-night reruns of *Full House*.

PART V

You're the Patron Saint of Lost Causes

I'm Sorry, We Don't Make Change

I Think My Ear Is Numb

Diminishing Returns

Two Become One?

1

I'm Sorry, We Don't Make Change

The question is whether you can and should change him. The answer is that only he can change himself, and if you can't accept him as he is, you should probably let him go.

Evan

Even if you think that you're perfect, pretty much everyone else would disagree. For example, I may feel that being friendly to the waitstaff is cute; you may want to kill me the next time I call our server by her first name. It's all subjective.

What is objective, however, is that, as part of a couple, you are bound to have issues with your partner, especially as the honeymoon luster begins to wear off. The women who say, "Jim isn't perfect, but he's perfect for me!"? Sorry. Nobody's perfect for anybody. What makes those cloying perfectionists a step wiser than the rest of us is not that they're perfectly matched, but that they've learned to accept their partner's imperfections. Let's say that you're dating one of those men who cuts the skin from the bottom of his feet with a nail clipper. There are going to be some women who roll their eyes and look away. There are going to be some women who laugh about it and offer to buy the guy a bigger nail clipper. And there are going to be some women who will see this behavior and ask for a divorce. Which one are you going to be? And if you happened to be the individual with the quirky habit, which person would you want your partner to be? I presume it's not the divorcé.

Men may be deeply flawed, but they are not your projects. So even if they're in need of a good tune-up and a complete paint job, unless they're bringing you in to be image consultants, please keep quiet about their perceived flaws. They probably know what their flaws are and, for better or worse, they accept them. If he's content with who he is, but you're not, you have two choices: stay or go. Sadly, it's the third option that some women tend to employ the most: nagging the shit out of them about all the things they do wrong until one of you can't take the tension anymore and calls the whole thing off.

Seems pretty obvious that choice #3 is the least desirable path, yet it's the most well-trod one. Why? I asked a female friend about this "men as projects" thing, and she said, "I think it's just that women are so conditioned by society to believe that we can't survive without men, that we need to be in love to be happy, that we do our best to stay in relationships and try to make everything as perfect as possible."

Are you buying this? I'm not. You wouldn't go into a church and try to convert the congregation to Islam. You wouldn't go to a country-western bar and ask the deejay to play 50 Cent. Then why are you compelled to take on the similarly impossible cause of trying to change a man?

Imagine you're dating a quiet guy. Your previous boyfriends were chatterboxes, manic-depressive roller coasters that attracted you at first, but ultimately wore you out. Now, after ten months with Mr. Stable, you're looking for more excitement, more passion, more drama. So what do you do? You start getting on him to be more gregarious at cocktail parties. You tell him that his silence is driving you crazy. You start fights to get reactions out of him. You let him know, in no uncertain terms, that his lack of communication skills is simply unacceptable.

What's a guy to do? Nothing. This is *who he is*. This is *who you fell in love with*. And now you're asking him to be somebody that he's not. I'm not suggesting that modifications can't be made for the sake of the relationship; I'm saying that while you can teach an old dog new tricks, you simply can't teach him to be a cat.

Linda

There are two different things going on in Evan's example. The futility of trying to alter a person's essence is a different issue than being overly picky about foot care.

As to why women try for the big changes, the reasons are fairly obvious when you've watched enough chick flicks. The cultural obsession with romantic love revolves in large part around the mostly false notion that it will make you someone else: the poor become rich, the ugly become beautiful, princesses literally rise from the fireplace ashes, and a frog is only a frog because he doesn't get enough smooches. There's a pretty powerful drive to be on either side of that myth—to find yourself miraculously transformed or to transform someone else.

In most cases, though, romantic ideas have a rather mundane flip side. Here, it's inertia. Giving up parts of your routine is always painful. People resist giving up relationships just like they do jobs and apartments. They stay too long when it's not working, and then they have so much sunk into it that they can't leave without feeling like they've lost whatever they invested. It's less wrenching to try to mold the person you have into the person you want than it is to throw yourself into being single again. So you get into an endless cycle of hunting for fixes that don't work because they can't work, and that's not fun for anybody.

To the degree that there's a sociological or psychological explanation for "men as projects," my sense is that this is an issue mostly for women who don't like themselves very much. They don't think anybody good is coming for them, and they certainly would never approach anyone good for fear of being cut off at the knees. But they don't want to be alone, either. So they pick a guy who's kind of a jackass and try to "bring him around" with the hope of winding up with someone good without having to upset the order of things too much. They believe that they will have, in a sense, beaten the system. It may be simplistic, but that has been my experience with the women I know. And, of course, have been.

So those are the big changes. What about the little nitpicks? I always suspect those things are ways of taking the temperature of the relationship. The objective isn't really to change the behavior, which, after all, doesn't matter. The objective, at least at some level, is to find out whether the guy will knock it off if you ask, essentially just because you ask. (Note that the associated stereotypically male behavior is nailing his feet to the floor about a perfectly reasonable and largely meaningless issue just to prove that *you are not the boss of him*.) These are tests, really, and tests are not a good idea.

Temptation lies in the fact that, every once in a while, people do change. In some cases, they change a lot. The problem is that they don't change *for other people*. Usually, the guy who picks you up at eight thirty is the same guy who's going to drop you off at two in the morning (unless you're drunk, in which case he may become slightly more alluring). What you meet is what you'll date, and what you're engaged to is what you'll be married to. It's fine to go out with people with problems, but if those problems are deal breakers for you, pick somebody else. Because people really, truly, honestly don't change for other people, and nobody deserves to be trapped in a relationship with somebody who expects them to apologize for who they are. It's a long trip, so take someone you at least believe you'll have fun with.

2

I Think My Ear Is Numb

You'll never talk a guy into wanting to talk when he doesn't.
Stereotypically, men don't feel the need to share as much. Re-
spect that or discover that he shuts down even more.

Evan

While doing my "research" for this book (namely, asking my guy friends, "What annoys you most about women?" during half-time of a Jets-Rams game), there was only one common sentiment that all my friends insisted be included: *"Please make them shut UP!"*

Earlier I talked about the whole Mars/Venus theory and how I didn't subscribe to it as a whole. Well, color me brown and pin a tail on me, because men and women really do have diametrically opposite takes on what it means to "communicate." So let's break it down—what most men think of the concept of overtalking—point by increasingly annoying point.

1. *There's great value in perspective.* When you want to deal with things NOW—not later, but NOW—you create a false sense of urgency. Ever have one of those moments where you thought of the perfect thing to say to him—ten hours after the fight? Think about it this way: If you'd instead waited ten hours to have that conversation, not only would it have been a calmer exchange of information, but maybe you could have used your great line. Or, better yet, maybe you wouldn't even have to bring out the big guns at all.

2. *We want to do what we want to do when we want to do it.* You could be talking about waking up in the morning, mowing the lawn, or ordering the lo mein, but men want to do things their way—even if your way makes a lot more sense. It's not right. It's not fair. It just is. Sometimes it's best to let him be a stubborn ass. Especially if you want him to make the same stubborn ass allowances for you from time to time.

3. *There are only so many ways to look at a problem.* Look at a card. There's a front and back. That's it. I'm not saying that everything is as simple as yes/no and black/white. I am saying that dealing with each individual "my boyfriend doesn't communicate well" situation as if it had all the complexities of a Middle East peace summit is a fast track to him never wanting to open his mouth again.

4. *Some problems literally have no solution.* So what's the point of laying it all out on the table when, in fact, all he wanted to do was go home after dinner instead of joining your friends for drinks? Is it *possible* that he can't stand your friends, that his attraction to you is waning, or that he's become a complete agoraphobic? Sure. Is it more likely that, as he said, he's just tired? Yup. Even if he's lying, I don't think the day has come when a woman has broken down a man due to intense questioning about a topic that is so thoroughly meaningless. More often than not, the best path is to accept him at his word, even if you don't believe him. Actually, let's flip it around. When we ask you if something is wrong and you tell us no, we're supposed to believe you, right? Oh. We're not? You mean you want us to keep on asking you the same question over and over in order to elicit a different response so that it's crystal clear that we're sensitive to your feelings? I see . . . Okay, then that part is different with men. No really means no.

5. *Nobody gains from this conversation.* If he doesn't want to talk, guess what? You're the only one who does. Any conversation at this point will not only be unproductive, but counterproductive. He has feelings, and even if you don't entirely understand them—even if *he* doesn't entirely understand them—you have to respect them. Getting a load off your chest has little intrinsic value to begin with, and that value goes down even further when you factor in that he *doesn't want to talk about it.*

A man can't fill your every need, and there are far worse things than falling for a man who is not fluent in chickspeak. That's for you to judge. Of course, we're not all heartless mutes, but if you're trying to turn your boyfriend into your girlfriend, you're fighting a very long uphill battle. There are men out there who like to communicate just like you do, and if you find one who's on your wavelength, grab him. Just make sure to budget time for a few marathon "let's talk about us" sessions every month. We love those.

Linda

It's a stereotype, of course, to say that women like to hash things out until every involved emotion has been identified, tagged, pinned to a Styrofoam board, placed under glass, and hung on the wall. It is also a stereotype to say that men want to discuss your average relationship issue for about twenty-six seconds, after which they will say, "Want to go eat?" But like most stereotypes, these contain some element of truth.

What if a guy balks at making time to talk, ever, even when it's important to you? Well then, that sucks, and it's on him, and you're not doing anything wrong to ask for that when it matters. Being allergic to relationship discussions is as silly as being addicted to them.

I'm talking about the other times. Like this: "What were you thinking before? No, really. No, really, what were you thinking? Because it seemed like you were going to say something, and then you didn't. You know, you can say it, I won't get mad. But seriously, what? I mean, I know that earlier you had been mad about the other thing, I mean, you said you weren't, but I could tell you were. I just feel like you won't even tell me now what you were thinking, and it makes me feel like you don't trust me or something, because this is what you always do, it's this thing, and it makes it really hard to . . . could you put down the magazine, actually?"

AIIIEEEEE! I don't even like this when people do it in friendships or in families. And that's *me*, and the last sentence I constructed from fewer than six clauses was probably written in crayon. You can imagine how crazy it might drive your boyfriend.

And not to get all tricky about it, but more than anything, this one is about strategy. It's not smart to teach the guy in your life that every feelings-related conversation is going to evolve into a production of *The Phantom of the Opera,* with the emoting and the singing and the swirling of capes. Because if you do, the next time it occurs to him to tell you he's in a crappy mood, he's going to decide against it. Because some part of him is going to think, *But "I'm in a crappy mood" will lead to "Why?" and I don't totally know why, and she'll think it's about her, and three hours from now we will still be talking about it, and that's when* Lost *is on.* And you will have missed a perfectly good opportunity for all that connecting you're craving.

Emotionally substantive conversations with men, I find, often work best as low-pressure, straightforward, not necessarily linear events. In fact, one of my closest male friends once hypothesized that Nintendo and backyard basketball hoops were both invented so that men could talk about their feelings. While you have the right to ask a guy to sit down and have a conversation on your terms, you should also be willing to talk the way guys often talk with each other; that is, while doing other things. I find that guys often will tell you all kinds of interesting stuff while, say, shoveling snow. Or walking to the store to get beer. Or theoretically discussing a movie. And you'll get a lot further with them—a *lot* further—if you don't plant your feet, turn to them, interrupt, and say, "That was very insightful! Let's talk more about that revelation!" Talk about a mood killer. There are guys with whom you have to be a little stealthy on the subject, I will admit.

Try not to have it be such an event. Have the talks you have to have, but train yourself not to need that constant stream of little reassurances that require interruptions of daily life for the purposes of having "sharing time." Worst-case scenario, you're going to become substantially better at Nintendo.

3

Diminishing Returns

Spending all day mooning over that married guy at your office? Secretly in love with your best friend? Waiting around for the guy who broke your heart ten years ago? Don't pour your energy into situations that will never, ever pay off; you'll have nothing left for situations that might.

Evan

Evan Marc Katz in the Martini Lounge. The evening is almost finished. Evan has had too much to drink. A woman in back raises her hand.

You have a question, ma'am?

"Yes. Why are men such assholes?"

Great question. I'm afraid we're running out of time, but we will be conducting a three-day seminar with that very title on Valentine's Day. Anybody else?

Yes, you, in the back, with the glasses.

"How do you know if a guy is being sincere when he shows interest?"

Well, as you know, there are many levels of interest. There's the idle compliment: "Gee, you look great today." There's the compliment with overtones: "What's that scent you're wearing? I love it." There's the request for face time that indicates it's just face time: "Let's grab lunch." There's the request for face time that indicates greater potential: "Let's grab drinks." Just know that none of these things mean diddly-squat. What does matter is what happens afterward. That's when you can tell where a guy's true intentions lie.

"What do you mean 'diddly-squat'? I don't compliment men on

their clothes or ask them to hang out just to be nice. Surely, a guy has to have some level of interest to say such things."

Granted, few men make overtures to the skinny girl with the buckteeth and the hair-net, but just asking for a date says little about his long term intentions. Stretched even further, he can sleep with you regularly and have absolutely no level of serious interest.

"Huh?! So a man invests time, energy, and money in somebody he doesn't even care about?"

Exactly.

"Wait, are you telling me that we can't even trust a guy who is thoughtful, funny, attentive, a good listener, and talks frequently about his desire for love and marriage?"

That's right. Just because a guy shows you a great time and seems sincere about finding a woman with whom he can share his life doesn't mean that he's interested in sharing his life with *you*.

"So if everything that he says means absolutely nothing, then how can a woman know where she stands with a guy?"

Friends, this is the heart of the matter. All that buttery stuff that he says every time you get together? Disregard it. It's what he does when he's *not* with you that counts most. Any guy can turn on the charm and tell you what you want to hear in the heat of the moment. Any guy can take the time to call you at eight o'clock on a Friday night on the off chance that you're around. Any guy can drop you an e-mail from time to time to keep his investment in you alive for just a little while longer. What separates the men from the boys—or, rather, the boyfriends from the players—is the effort he makes to follow up. Guys who are interested in you will call the next day to tell you they had a great time. They will not get off the phone until they've set another date to get together. Sure, there are exceptions. But even if he's going on a two-week business trip, his last question to you should be, "What night are you available when I get back?" If, for some inexplicable reason, you're waiting for him to ask you out, and he hasn't, the writing is on the wall.

"Maybe it's just me, but you're missing something essential

here, Evan. It's not like I'm completely in the dark and think that a guy is in love with me when he isn't. It's more that I think he could be one day. If we have a great connection, isn't it possible that it's just a matter of time?"

Listen, it's not my place to suggest that every unrequited love will remain unrequited forever. It's not my place to suggest that the women who actually have a clue are as foolish as the women who are clueless. All I can say is that, regardless of your level of self-awareness, the solution is the same when it comes to the guy who isn't stepping up to the plate. Move on.

If you dropped an apple fifty times and it fell every time, you'd probably expect it to hit the ground on the fifty-first try as well. Women who harbor hopes for a future with a man who doesn't share her desire are hoping, in essence, that gravity takes a holiday. They steadfastly refuse to look at the situation as an objective observer, all because they don't truly want to face the facts. It's a shame.

To borrow two clichés: The truth hurts. But it will also set you free.

Linda

Oh, the gift of perseverance is such a pain in the ass, isn't it?

I could open here with a hundred different "let me tell you about a time when I was extremely stupid" stories, but here's one executive summary: I adored a deeply screwed-up guy for a number of years whose version of eventually confessing his feelings for me was to drunkenly tell me (in front of a roomful of people) that he had been battling his attraction to me for long enough that he certainly wasn't going to give in to it now. And because life is not an Ethan Hawke movie, he never did. Instead, he drifted away, got arrested, and vanished, but you can imagine how much better I felt after attaining the brass ring by waiting around until he finally confessed. Yeah . . . not really.

There's a certain irony, I think, in concluding a years-long march through a hopeless, depressing nightmare of a nonrelationship by telling yourself that at least you know you're not crazy. Because in reality, it's exactly crazy, hanging around forever, knowing at some level that the game you're playing just isn't going to pay off, ever. You can play this one out in a number of ways. They all look different, but they're all the same. The married guy, the compulsive dater who uses you as the emergency backup girl, the guy who screwed you over a long time ago who you are convinced will one day wake up and figure out that he never should have let you get away—these are games you are doomed to lose before you start playing.

So why do you keep it up? For one thing, after a certain amount of figurative blood has been spilled, your investment is such that you want something. You just want *something*. I mean, in the end, what I got from the guy in that story, whether he was telling the truth or screwing with me, was a kick in the teeth. I would have been much better off with nothing. But because I wouldn't sit down, do the math, and cut my losses, I waited around until I got the kick. You could argue that, in all likelihood, nothing but the kick was going to end it because of the way my heels were dug in.

Furthermore, the fact that the situation will never pay off doesn't mean the guy isn't playing. While some guys in these situations are pretty much blameless, others are haunted by plenty of bullshit of their own, and once they learn (from you) what it takes to keep you on the hook, they're going to keep squeaking out that minimum effort, expending as little energy as possible because that's all it takes. And every time you think about cutting them loose, they'll again cough up a pitiful little scrap that's perfectly calibrated to keep the dance going and make sure you don't leave.

So, knowing that, if you like the dance, then, by all means, keep doing it. But what you shouldn't do is convince yourself all that dancing means he has any degree of genuine affection for you, because it doesn't. The fact that the guy doesn't want you to get any farther away than you are doesn't mean he's ever going to let you any closer, either. He may just leave you in that very lonely place, right where you've been for months or years, for as long as you're willing to stay.

And unlike a lot of things you'll confront, *it doesn't matter why*. You're going to want to understand it. "I can tell that he . . . so why won't he . . . because he . . . and then he . . ." Yeah. Just stop. It's a seductive game, trying to figure out what's going on in somebody else's head, but it's a drop-dead terrible idea. First of all, your odds of ever really cracking anybody else's code are relatively small. Even if you do, your insight doesn't give you options as when you have it about yourself. Figuring out how *you* operate is—up to a point—useful, because if you figure out what you're doing wrong, you can make different choices. But let's say your hard-fought insight is actually correct, and the compulsive dater treats you like the emergency backup girl only because he's insecure, and thus constantly needs new girlfriends to pump up his ego, despite the fact that somewhere in the dark recesses of his mind he wants you desperately. Let's say you're right. So what? What are you going to do about it? "I'll tell him!" Yeah, that'll teach him. And if you're very lucky, you'll "win" the affections of someone so emotionally underdeveloped that he's terrified to acknowledge his own feelings without the intervention of a cattle prod. What a treat.

It should be obvious by now that I'm not against trying to understand other people. What I *am* against is lingering in a situation that does nothing but make you miserable just because you've figured out that it's all his mom's fault, or his old girlfriend's fault, or the fault of his being a frustrated poet. Whatever the reason, someone who gives you nothing will probably continue to give you nothing, right up until the point where you walk away. And you have to walk away. *Not* to teach him a lesson, *not* to drive him to an epiphany, and *not* to provoke a resolution. You walk away because *he gives you nothing,* and, by definition, a relationship with him is a losing proposition for you. Hang around waiting for the kick in the teeth, and you'll probably get it.

4

Two Become One?

You're not going to want to do everything together, you're not going to like all the same movies, and you're not going to agree on every significant issue in current affairs. Don't insist on a complete brain merge, and don't feel restless when you don't get one.

Evan

"You complete me." These three words are as dangerous as "Eat this anthrax" or "I have crabs."

You know those couples who are truly inseparable? The ones who used to be called "Bill" and "Tina" and are now known as the single entity "Billntina." Because she comes to his poker nights. And he comes to the movies with her girlfriends. And she keeps all her clothes at his place. And he can't go out for a drink after work without asking her. And you think, Wow, I've never seen two people so attached at the hip in my life. And you think, Wow, wouldn't it be nice to have someone there for me all the time? And you think, Wow, I think I'd slit my wrists if someone followed me around like a shadow, even if he was my favorite person in the world.

Have you ever dated some guy who was on you like white on rice and asked yourself as he wrapped himself around you at night, "What the hell did this guy do before I came into the picture? It's like his life just started the day he spilled a vodka tonic on me near the jukebox." Isn't that just plain *weird*? Yeah, we think so, too.

The primary reason for expanding your interests beyond, say, him, is that you're most likely suffocating him, but he hasn't had a moment to himself to think about how to break it to you. If he wants your company when he goes grocery shopping, he'll ask you. Otherwise, just let him go by himself. It doesn't mean he's mad at you, it doesn't mean he's moody, it doesn't mean he's an inaccessible loner. It just means he wants to pick up his S'Mores Pop-Tarts without hearing how Weetabix is better for him.

These are the things you need to know about men. Sometimes we need to drive alone. Sometimes we don't want to answer questions before we go to sleep. Sometimes we need to spend the night in our own beds. Sometimes we want to play softball without having to worry about paying attention to you. Sometimes it's really, really nice to hear you say that you're going out for drinks with the girls from work or, better yet, that you're taking a weekend to visit your mom in Massachusetts and you don't want us to come with you this time.

Don't get me wrong. I never meant to suggest that it's impossible to be happy with just one person in your life or to intimate that you're a loser if you don't do ladies' night out once a month. But it does seem pretty obvious that if you invest every single ounce of your energy in him, it leaves you nothing left for you. And if you can imagine the remote possibility that he may not always be right there by your side, wouldn't it be smart to have a more solid foundation of your own?

Think about it this way: Romantic relationships are risky tech stocks. Platonic relationships are (relatively) stable mutual funds. Better to diversify now than to realize after the crash that everything you invested in is gone.

Linda

Oh, *these* people. The "I was nothing before you" people. The "my life began the day we met" people. The "I carry your name in my heart, as well as having it tattooed on my ass" people. The "I wear your blood in a vial around my neck" people. Yeah, these people are nuts.

Look, everybody wants the love of her life to be transformative. Everybody wants to give adequate respect to the awe-inspiring set of feelings you get from that person who excites you to such a degree that it feels like you might actually combust. But, ultimately, you are still you, and the odds are that you're not going to marry yourself. Sure, you know couples who met because they both listed some obscure piece of Finnish anime as their favorite movie, or because they're both passionately devoted to sea monkeys or blue Kool-Aid. But that's not most people. Most people are attracted to each other for reasons that are a little bit more complicated than that, and what that means is that your beloved is very unlikely to share all your particular quirks.

Take your preferences in something like movies. As it happens, one of my close friends is a fan of chick movies, while her husband is a fan of Steven Seagal and such. Her favorite movies are films like *The Goodbye Girl*; his favorite movies are films like *Tremors*. They could theoretically waste a huge amount of time sitting around trying to find something that they agree on. Not too girly; not too sweaty. Not too ponderous; not too loud. Not too hard or too soft, too fast or too slow . . . and they might find something. But neither one of them would get what he or she really wants. She'd miss the sappy date movies, and he'd fall behind in the exploding helicopters genre. What's a couple to do?

In their case, they alternate. They go to see one of his movies, and then they go to one of hers. And yes, they both lose out half the time by seeing movies they otherwise wouldn't. But they also both win half the time, and meanwhile, they're at the movies together, which is sort of the point. Going alone, of course, is an option. Waiting for the video is an option. There are a variety of ways to handle the situation. Bad options, I think, would include giving up movies, deciding that their divergent tastes mean they aren't a good match, fighting endlessly, or getting into a secret, passive-aggressive game in which the same person always gives in and then sits around feeling resentful.

Honestly, the need to appear to be one person has always struck me as a bit of a crutch. Look at the grand gestures celebrities take to show off to the public the perfection of their relationships. Okay, you're not Tom Cruise on *Oprah* jumping on the couch, but when you have to show off how inseparable you are, it has the same hint of desperation.

I see nothing to fear from a woman having her own life separate from everyone else, including her boyfriend. She goes out to dinner with her best friend; he goes over to a friend's house to watch football; everybody comes home at the end of the evening; everybody's happy. What's the problem? What would you gain from refusing to allow either one of you any breathing room?

If a guy is treating his relationship with you like a leash, then that's the problem, and it really doesn't matter whether you let him off that leash periodically or not. Trying to create a perfectly unified life in order to convince yourself and everyone else that your boyfriend no longer exists as an independent person capable of leaving you is an exercise in futility.

Your relationship is going to have to weather the fact that there are a whole lot of things in the world that could theoretically be distractions or outright threats. You can settle in with the guy, you can marry the guy, and at some point he's going to meet someone he might have married if he hadn't married you. (The same thing, incidentally, will probably happen to you.) Because people continue to exist. They don't collapse into couple-monsters. No matter how joined at the hip you appear to be, you're not. If you stay together, it's because you're choosing to, even though he isn't you, and doesn't always speak directly from inside your head, and doesn't always want to do what you're doing. In fact, making that choice every day always strikes me as more romantic than a shared interest in sea monkeys.

PART VI

You Fight Like a Girl

Everything You Say Can and Will Be
Used Against You

———

Boyfriends with Boy (and Girl)
Friends

———

I Just Love Your Shoes!

———

Get Over It

1

Everything You Say Can and Will Be Used Against You

You say just as many stupid things (okay, maybe not), but men forget about them because SportsCenter *pushes them out of their limited memories. You don't have to forget, but you really must forgive.*

Evan

I've got a joke. Ready?

"Do I look fat in these jeans?"

What do you mean that's not a joke? It is to us. Think about all the ways that question can be answered by a man. The possibilities are endless. As long as the first word is "No." Any man who has ever started with any other word is still paying for it. Thus the title of this chapter.

There are lots of stupid things that we say, most of which you could probably recount for us given a free Sunday or something. Whatever it is, we know you're listening, because anything that we've ever said that is less than flattering to us or to you is etched on your brain like the Ten Commandments.

There's a statute of limitations on violent crimes, and there should likewise be a time to stop dredging up dirt about our partners. This is not to say that there aren't factors which should make you wary about entering a relationship, but once you're there, it's wrong to hold these very sensitive, very personal things against your partner.

Generally, however, it's the little things that bug you most and always come back to haunt us. This is not a defense of *anything* we said. Again, we're starting with the premise that men say stupid things so routinely it's as if making verbal gaffes is a function as essential as breathing. The moral of the story is—as it has been in a number of chapters—So fucking what?

So we think your best friend from high school is annoying and really needs to lose the cardigan sweaters. So we once hooked up with our older, divorced neighbor while her two children were asleep upstairs. So we didn't really like your short story about your fifth-grade boyfriend who gave you that papier-mâché Spider-Man doll. What does any of this have to do with anything going on *right now*?

The fact is, we're gonna slip up. We confess that your mom was looking old last night, that your new haircut isn't as nice as the old one, or that we have absolutely no interest in spending time with you at antique stores. Are we wrong for feeling this way? Nah. Are we stupid to tell you "the truth" when we know it'll probably hurt you? Yep. Really stupid. Because once we say it, it's out there. It lives and breathes and might as well be written down on a card for you to carry in your back pocket for eternity.

Just do us a favor: Put away the card.

Nobody gains from the kind of interactions that begin with the words, "You once said." You once said? I once said that I thought I could fly—when I was seven. I once said that it was of paramount importance to be popular—when I was sixteen. I would hope nobody would hold me to either one. Nobody in a relationship should have to be a cautious politician, wary of speaking, for fear of their words being held against them. That's no way to live.

If, as they say, actions speak louder than words, judge us for them instead. Because if we are nice to your best friend, and have no desire to cheat, and soldier on gamely while you hold up dusty candelabras, it shouldn't make a difference. We're happy to be with you and are willing to put up with all the things that we don't like so we can continue being with you. If we had more than a tissue-thin filter between our brains and mouths, we'd never had said that stuff at all, but we don't, so let us be, okay?

P.S. If we're still interested in sex, the way you look in those jeans doesn't matter to us at all. This has been a public service announcement paid for by men.

Linda

Oh, we do love to parse, we really do. Not all of us; not the ones of us who have enough experience with guys in enough different situations to know that the answer to "What did that *meeeean*?" is usually "Nothing," but lots of us, we love to parse.

Because you're seeing him tomorrow, and yesterday he said, "I can't wait to see you," and then today he said, "I'm looking forward to it," and that kind of seems like going backward, doesn't it? Because "can't wait" is happier than "looking forward," so why is he less excited today than he was yesterday? And then he sent the one e-mail that was signed "Love," but then the next one was signed "Best," and what the hell is "Best," anyway? "Best" is for fucking business correspondence! You sign "Best," and then you attach your résumé!

And then there was that time when you were going to go to the movies, and an hour before you were going to leave, he said that thing about how he thinks American movies aren't any good anymore. Couldn't he have been a little bit excited since this was less than twenty-four hours after the huge blowup about the dishes and the thing with your mother? *You would think he would know* that being all unenthusiastic about the movie would hurt your feelings because you're the one who suggested it in the first place.

I used to run my guy-related questions past one of my male friends, and whenever I would say, "Well, here's what he said; what do you think that means?" the answer was almost always the same. He would say, "I guarantee you that by asking me about this, you have already thought about it much harder than he did when he said it." And it's true. An awful lot of the time, when you're wondering what something means, it's not that you don't deserve to know, and it's not that it's intrusive for you to ask, and it's not that you shouldn't take the answer too much to heart. It's that there literally isn't an answer. People say things. And as Evan pointed out, much of the time, it just means what it means. The proposition stands for itself. "I got a DUI once" means "I got a DUI once." "Your mom was driving me crazy with that Johnny Mathis shit" means just that.

Not only do many things contain only their literal meaning, but many things contain absolutely no meaning whatsoever. What does it mean that he signs an e-mail like this instead of like that? Most of the time, *not a damn thing*.

I think women have a way of speaking in small gestures and tiny, almost imperceptible signals. Accordingly, we cling to small remarks like talismans for years and years and years because we convince ourselves that every remark has some sort of meaning, and our task is to find it. It stands to reason then, that a guy who says a remark means nothing is keeping something from you. Thus is a simple communication issue transformed into a trust issue, or one of those horrible woman-as-therapist situations where you feel like you're supposed to go spelunking into the guy's soul to figure out what in the hell he's talking about. And the whole time, it means *nothing*. There's nothing to figure out. It's Geraldo and Al Capone's vault all over again, and there's still nothing in there but dusty old bottles.

It's not that guys aren't tricky, and it's not that they're not obtuse—because, oh man, they can be. But if you're dragging out a single comment from last year because you've just always been so curious about it, then knock it off. He probably doesn't even re-member saying it, let alone have any clue what it means. Save your-self the trouble and wipe your brain clean like an Etch A Sketch. The ability to shrug is at least as important as the ability to dig.

2

Boyfriends with Boy (and Girl) Friends

Most guys come with a battery of friends, some of whom you may not adore, and some of who may be women. You can (1) embrace them, (2) get them on your team, or (3) wait for them to come up with an unflattering nickname for you. The last of these strategies is not recommended.

Evan

Imagine you had a wonderful boyfriend who you really loved who just happened to hate your best friend. In fact, he hated her so deeply that he felt the need to make prank phone calls late at night to her home. Sure, it's an outlandish hypothetical, but it illustrates a favorite unwritten rule of mine: If forced to choose between two people, and only one of them is being psychotic, the decision is a no-brainer.

Usually, however, such instances aren't so clear-cut. Suppose you're the new girlfriend and there are no prank calls, but you've exchanged a few snarky remarks with his roommate. Or maybe you get along famously with his guy friends, but you really can't stand his omnipresent ex-girlfriend. Or perhaps he's part of a tight-knit group from college that has seen a lot of his girlfriends come and go, so they're not too willing to embrace you until they see that you're a keeper. Whatever it is, there are always going to be barriers in the way of having a perfectly harmonious fit with his friends. And why not? Though you love your boyfriend, you two don't agree on everything; it only stands to reason that you're not going to like everyone in his life. Not anymore than you like everyone at your office. Or in your family. And let's be honest; there are a few of your own friends that you're not so crazy about, either.

You know the cliché that states when you marry someone, you're also marrying his family? Well, that's what you're up against with his friends. And since you can never get rid of his catty mom, why hold any illusions that his annoying summer camp pals are going to disappear anytime soon?

See, the transitive property doesn't apply to friendships. Just because Nancy likes Billy and Billy likes Tommy doesn't mean Nancy's going to like Tommy. More likely, Nancy is going to think that Tommy is (a) a loser, (b) a stupid frat boy, (c) an alcoholic womanizer, or (d) a misogynist who is a bad influence on her boyfriend. Actually, it's probably (e) all of the above. Doesn't matter. Because even if Nancy's 100 percent correct, her negative feelings do little besides cause friction between her and Billy. Ultimately, Billy is only going to jettison Tommy if he feels that he detracts from his life more than he adds to it. If he chooses to go down with the S.S. *Loser,* he's not going to be receptive to you throwing him a life preserver.

Let's flip our perspective. Have you ever considered that he has to spend equal time hanging out with some of your friends who he's not crazy about? Well, if you don't want him to carp that he has to listen to Marie yammer on about her workout routine, maybe you should just can it about his buddy Adam's pathetic quest for a threesome. He's always going to be more forgiving of his friends. You'll always be more forgiving of yours. Friends by association or inheritance simply aren't the same as two people who have forged genuine bonds over the years.

But so what? You can't choose your workmates, you can't choose your in-laws, and you definitely can't choose your boyfriend's friends. If you find that you just can't get along with his posse, there's a simple solution: Make yourself scarce when his friends are around. Better yet, make his friend time the same as your friend time.

Friday nights are boys' night out *and* girls' night out. That way, the only time anyone will ever have to play nice is when you're pairing up the bridesmaids and groomsmen. And at that point, I have no doubt that such good friends will all be on their best behavior.

Linda

We've already agreed that you shouldn't date men who have no lives, because they tend to be boring and unhappy, and that's no fun for anyone. Of course, we're not recommending that you date men who have wives or girlfriends, because . . . okay, if that one's not obvious, read the entire book over from the beginning. I'll wait. So if you're seeking someone who has an active, happy life not based around being part of a couple, where does that leave you? With the friends. Oh, the friends. Apart from those who are entirely antisocial, everybody's got them, everybody loves them, and they're going to be part of the picture, whether you like them or not.

The optimist's view of your boyfriend's friends, of course, is that they are potential friends for you. Roughly speaking, you like him and he likes them, so there's a decent chance that you're going to find common ground with them. And please, don't judge based on a single meeting whether that's going to be true or untrue. I've certainly been in the position of explaining my friends' behavior from time to time after the creation of an imperfect first impression. "She's really not like that, usually." "She's better in one-on-one situations." And the best one of all: "Yeah, I don't know what that was." A lot of people genuinely are bad in groups, nervous with strangers, or socially inept in some strange and wonderful way that you'll find endearing once you adjust to it. So be patient.

Of course, that doesn't mean it won't be uncomfortable at first. If nothing else, some closely bonded groups of friends are just hard to break into in ways that have nothing to do with you. When you walk into a roomful of people who have known each other for ten years, you miss a good percentage of what's going on. You don't know the history, you don't know the inside jokes, and you don't know who knocked out whose teeth on the Fourth of July in 1998. You feel excluded, in a sense, because you *are* excluded.

I am of the opinion that the worst thing you can possibly do in that situation is overexert yourself. Intrusiveness breeds defensiveness, and phony, forced bonds aren't going to take, anyway. Try to wedge your way into the middle of a crowd like that and you'll see them cringe. It's not to say you can't hope for the best, but you can't be freaked out if it doesn't happen for you.

If you ask me, the best strategy is to keep meetings intimate. It's really better to start out in a couple of small-scale settings where only one or two other people are involved, but even if you absolutely have to meet the entire throng all at once, there's a fairly good chance that somebody will take pity on your foundering self. When that happens, don't pass it up. If somebody tries to talk to you in the kitchen while you're grabbing a Diet Coke, talk back. Once you've got one ally, the rest is cake. Not only will this give you somebody to talk to, but when they're all sitting around talking about you later—and they will—if everybody else says, "I don't know; I didn't really talk to her," you want there to be one person who can say, "I talked to her; she was cool."

There's one other thing about this guy that you're seeing. Some of his friends may be women. Some of them may be women he likes a lot. Some of those women may be better-looking than you are, or funnier than you are, or they may share some interest of his that you don't. I'm not going to tell you that it's impossible that any of these women present a threat to you, because if I did, everyone would be able to come up with counterexamples of the "they swore they were just friends, *but then, of course . . .*" variety. Like a lot of other things, it's a time to play the odds. Whatever they told you in *When Harry Met Sally . . .*, the odds are that if the guy is otherwise trustworthy, what is presented to you as a platonic friendship is a platonic friendship. And if that's the case, if you get all shirty about it, pursing your lips and complaining and undermining, you're going to (1) piss off the guy, (2) piss off the friend, and (3) make a very poor impression on his other friends, who are probably also friends with her. Getting tagged with that label, that you're jealous and threatened by every relationship he has, is not something you want to have happen.

Furthermore, the ability to have platonic female friends, in my experience, speaks very well of guys. Guys who are incapable of having female friends likely single-mindedly think of all women as potential sex partners, have heavy loads of sexist bullshit kicking around in their heads, or have something else holding them back. If your boyfriend has platonic women friends, it's because he relates to women in a basically healthy, normal, positive way. This is a good thing. Don't fight it.

3

I Just Love Your Shoes!

Stepping outside yourself and into his position is the single best way to understand where he's coming from and thus avert many recurring relationship issues.

Evan

Any man you're going to date is going to have a whole lot of life experience informing his decisions. Which means that even if you are incredibly compatible with him—same value system, similar life goals, complementary star signs—there are *always* going to be things upon which you disagree. As I see it, your options are as follows:

1. *Insist that you're right and he's wrong.* Hear that? It's your future ticking away slowly as you wait for him to come around to your definitively correct point of view.

2. *Concede that he's right even if you're convinced that he's wrong.* Watch your resentment bubble over like a box of Tide in a washing machine as you attempt to fall asleep beside him.

3. **Ask him to explain himself further.* Listen to his explanation. Accept his explanation even if you don't agree with it. End fight on the spot.

One of the stupidest arguments I ever got into took place after a formal party I attended with my girlfriend. When we arrived

*the right answer

outside my friend's casual house party, I was dressed in a tuxedo. I'd come prepared with a change of clothes because there was *no way* I was entering this roomful of guys in jeans and T-shirts dressed like a mâitre d'. No matter how much guys may love each other's company, they love making fun of each other even more. Given that, I wanted to change in the car. My girlfriend thought I was being silly and insisted that I go up to the party and change in my friend's bathroom. We were at an impasse—a remarkably absurd, low-stakes impasse. Was I making too big a deal about being mocked by my friends? Probably. Was she being equally unreasonable for not understanding my idiosyncratic sensitivity? According to irrational Evan, at the time: Yeah. And so voices were raised and feelings were hurt and connections were bruised, all because I'd rather change in a car than put up with a little ribbing and because she didn't want to let me have my way.

I bring this up knowing that it makes me look like an idiot. But sometimes—or, often, in my case—you have to look like an idiot to learn a valuable lesson. And the lesson I learned was not that my friends wouldn't make fun of me—because when they saw me going upstairs in my penguin suit, they certainly did—but that there are many situations in which it's pointless to square off against each other. Even if I was the silly one, my girlfriend turned it into a drama by not just letting me be silly. Since there was no realistic way of convincing me that I was overreacting, why not just let me overreact?

The point is not that I couldn't just as easily have given in and sucked it up; I think it's about determining which party thinks it's a bigger deal. Sometimes he'll overreact, sometimes you'll overreact—but every time, one of you has to step aside and let the other person "win." After all, that's what compromise *is*.

Being agreeable—admittedly not my strong suit—is often the best way to tackle differences of opinion. If your coworker is in a tizzy about the copy machine, it's valuable to consider how frustrating it can be for her. If your mom is going on and on about the way you're driving on the center stripe, it's useful to empathize with her fear. If your friend seems irrationally agitated about the way some cashier looked at her, it's best just to smile and nod. Absent full understanding, you must resign yourself to the fact that people will always surprise you. If you can't acknowledge the validity of another person's point of view, skip the relationship and run for Congress. You'll fit in perfectly.

Linda

I would take issue with the idea that men are reliably being agreeable and understanding with that blank stare, as opposed to, say, not paying attention, but the idea remains the same. And the idea is that genuinely putting yourself in the other person's position doesn't just mean trying to figure out how *you* would react in the same situation. A person's reactions are the sum of her history and personality and all of that, so trying to put yourself entirely in someone else's position will only make you come out in the same place she did.

You can't precisely duplicate what it's like to be your boyfriend. What I think makes more sense is to try to hear and credit—basically on faith—the way the guy is saying that *he* feels. It's not that you have to accept or go along with unreasonable demands made on you or give up on the idea of being able to sympathize. You may not sympathize with the guy's position in a particular situation, but you can probably sympathize with what it's like to feel lousy. Taken from that perspective, whether it sounds logical to you or not, something that makes your boyfriend miserable or makes him feel really small and crappy is probably something he shouldn't be doing. Nobody deserves that. I think that sometimes, along with the responsibility women often feel for doing the emotional work in their relationships, there comes a certain dismissiveness, as if women are genetically destined to be the "experts" on matters involving people's emotions. It can make them prone to confidently diagnose feelings they don't agree with as manifestations of guilt, passive-aggressiveness, hostility, fear of commitment, or insecurity, and, ultimately, you can't do that.

Besides, as we've said about a bunch of other things, it almost always doesn't matter. When the situation calls for it, you ought to be willing to surrender the point *just because*. Suppose a guy's position about something is based on irrational insecurities. Sure, if the "something" is having kids, or spending money, or buying a house, or monogamy, then you have to crack that open and figure it out, because it's too important to let it go. But if you secretly suspect that insecurity is making him really, really not want to, say, go to a particular party with you—it's not making him stay in like a hermit, it's just making him want to skip an event one time—then, who cares? Honestly, *who cares?* If the issue isn't significant, the fact that letting him off the hook will make him feel good rather than bad is reason enough. It's an act of love to allow people to be momentarily foolish without forcing them to empty their pockets emotionally and show you everything they've got.

This isn't even a rule of dating, really, or a rule of men and women. This is a rule of people. People feel the way they feel. They want to go on vacation, or they don't. They want to change jobs, or they don't. And, ultimately, when you drill down into the heart of all this, they love you or they don't. And if you believe they love you, it tends to make you brave and generous, because their moments of madness don't really threaten you. You can allow them a wide berth about the things you know they react to differently than you would. Perhaps they are quicker to end friendships than you would be. Perhaps they get angry more or less quickly, or about different things. Even if you can't entirely find your way into their shoes, you can take their word for it when they tell you what makes their feet hurt.

4

Get Over It

Remember how, as a child, you'd instantly forget about an argument you had with your sister in the backseat of the car? Do the same thing now. Holding a grudge has never helped a relationship.

Evan

Everything I've learned about conflict resolution, I learned from Kenny Rogers. I remember one night back in 1977: I was lost, hitting the bottle, causing problems at home. Of course, I was five years old, so you could say that I didn't know better, but Kenny wouldn't let me off the hook. At that point, he was known mostly for his 1974 hit "Lucille." But as the beer flowed and the clock ticked, and I talked about how I'd been fighting with my old lady, Kenny laid it all out for me as plain as the Texas summer sky.

"You've got to know when to hold 'em, know when to fold 'em."

Translation: If you're on the losing end of an argument, you better learn to shut the hell up and apologize.

A girlfriend of mine was really stressing about what kind of dress to wear to a friend's wedding. It was on a Sunday afternoon in August, so black was out, red was too showy, and white was an obvious no-no. She ended up choosing a hot-looking lavender silk number, which made us both very happy . . . until we walked in and saw that she was dressed like all the bridesmaids.

That wasn't the real problem. The real problem was that I laughed. Mostly because it was funny. Maybe a part of me thought that we could joke our way past this minor inconvenience, especially since there was nothing we could do about it. Uh uh. Not only was my girlfriend traumatized by the wardrobe similarity, but my jocular manner dug me a hole the size of the Grand Canyon. After a couple of minutes of trying to get her to see the lighter side of the situation, I realized that the only thing I could do was apologize profusely and empathize with her plight. A few days and a whole lot of tears later, we made up. Yet if had I remembered Kenny's advice from the get-go, I could have saved us both a whole lot of trouble.

"Know when to walk away, know when to run."

Translation: If you can't agree to disagree, you're in for some very long nights staring at the ceiling or sleeping on the couch.

Explanation: Agreeing to disagree is the single most important part of Getting Over It, because there is no arbitrator that's going to step in and award you points just because you're 65 percent right and he's 35 percent right. Even if there were, even if you tallied up all the argument points that you've ever won over your hapless, ill-informed boyfriend, what would you possibly do with them? Nothing. "Winning" arguments takes as much time as winning 3,000 Skee-Ball tickets—and has about the equivalent value. So unless a handful of spider rings and Superballs are important to you, it's generally best to just leave it alone.

"You never count your money when you're sittin' at the table / There'll be enough for countin' when the dealin's done."

Translation: Congratulations, you won the fight. Now be a gracious winner and never bring up the topic again.

Explanation: Sometimes things *are* clear-cut. He started a fight with a guy at the movies. He got drunk and made a fool out of himself at a dinner party. He forgot that you had plans for dinner and left you waiting for two hours. In such instances, he has no justifiable excuse. This doesn't mean he won't try to invent one, and it doesn't mean he can't cobble together something that sounds semireasonable. But whatever his motives, his actions were wrong, and he's gotta step up and apologize. And you, class act that you are, have to accept his apology and let it go. No allusions to past disagreements. No storing up ammunition for future battles. And certainly no passive-aggressive comments. You're right, he's wrong, move on!

A couple I know have their share of marital squabbles. One evening, the day after a touchy argument that they had agreed was patched up, the husband came home with two bouquets of flowers. Despite the "peace" that they had made and the floral gesture, the wife remained as pissy and stone-faced as if he had just skinned her cat. Not good. After you make up, you have to let things go, especially in front of other people. I know another couple in which the wife constantly berated her husband for his career choice (writer), although she married him knowing full well his chosen vocation. Not only did her negative jibes surely affect his confidence, but it made everyone around them terribly uncomfortable.

Of course, the word "sorry" does not heal all, nor do a couple of bouquets of flowers, but what more can you possibly do once everything has been said? What value is there in hashing out the same issue over and over again?

It's one thing to be all about sharing feelings and another thing to always beat a dead horse into some ugly, sticky glue. I would never compare your precious relationship with horse-based glue, but Kenny would, and since he's been happily married since 1997, I think you should listen to him.

Linda

There's such a thing as a healthy grudge. I bear healthy grudges against (1) my bank, (2) the Columbia House Music Club, (3) a guy who once told me a truckload of lies, causing havoc that took years to untangle, (4) a vet who didn't properly care for a cat of ours and later sniped that it was because he was too busy to give us all the relevant information, (5) one of my college professors, (6) Justice Scalia, and (7) a kid who regularly plagiarizes my writing on the Internet. I dislike all these people and entities based on their past (and, in some cases, ongoing) misdeeds, and I do not deny it. I won't be getting over it, I won't cotton to any platitudes about bygones, and if I see any of them walking down the street, I will flash them a dirty look like you would not believe. Not that you can really see the Columbia House Music Club walking down the street, but you get the idea. I learned a long time ago that the ability to live peacefully in a universe in which you have enemies will save you years of misery.

But grudges against people you're supposed to love, or like, or be related to? Those are not so healthy. The great thing about being angry at my college professor is that I never have to see him again. In fact, I don't feel the need to achieve resolution of my feelings in any of those cases, and I don't feel the need to be forgiving. Why would I forgive the vet? He never apologized. The hell with him! My cat died! Bad vet!

But when you feel like you've been wronged by somebody you care about, it's sort of like singing "Row, Row, Row Your Boat," in that everybody knows how to keep it going, and nobody knows the graceful way to end it. And if you don't end it, you will wind up having the same relationship with your boyfriend that I have with my bank. And, believe me, you do not want that to happen.

Of course, the way you put away your anger depends partly on what you have to work with. If you get lucky, you'll have an honest conversation about it. You'll work out whatever caused the fight and feel comfortable that the problem is solved. The biggest hazard is probably "winning" the argument—which you will do from time to time, in the sense of extracting a flat-out, unqualified apology—and then feeling the need to go back and "teasingly" bring it up over and over again—which you should not do. Unless you enjoy being reminded of everything you've ever done wrong, shut up and forget it.

Things are naturally more difficult when you expend a lot of effort, and when it's over, you still don't feel like you've solved anything. You've been offered a dubious explanation, or you still think he was wrong and he still thinks you were wrong, and no amount of discourse has changed anyone's mind. What to do?

Sometimes, the smartest thing is to ask yourself this: What is the worst thing that will happen if I resolve to never think about this again? Women—especially women who have never had close, platonic male friends—wildly underestimate the prominence of "Oh my God, would you fucking *drop it*" in the list of male complaints about women. If I were to pick out one area in which men have us at a disadvantage, it would be that of not thinking and talking the life out of everything that happens until everyone involved is a dried-out husk. I once got into a fairly heated e-mail exchange with a male friend who worked in my office, and it went on all morning, and then, at about eleven, he sent me one that said, "We have to be friends again by eleven thirty because, remember, that's when we have to leave for lunch." And we were. Ding! Fight over. Because it didn't really matter, and when it doesn't really matter, you can just declare it over. And it is. You can even shout "Ding!" if you want, but make sure the guy knows what you're talking about or you'll get funny looks.

PART VII

You're Boring Him in the Bedroom

The Beauty Myth Is Not a Myth

———

Who Are You and What Did You Do with My Girlfriend?

———

Good Girls Don't

1

The Beauty Myth Is Not a Myth

It's not much fun to report than men actually are as shallow as advertised. Awareness and acceptance of this should hopefully temper your frustration (or lack thereof) with the opposite sex.

Evan

I took one of those attraction tests online and was shocked to learn that my physical tastes were classified as "very selective." In other words, 98 percent of all men are apparently more open than I am when it comes to a woman's looks. For a guy who thinks of himself as generally nonjudgmental and self-aware, this is an embarrassing result.

The truth, as it always does, lies somewhere in between. The test asked what I found attractive, and, not surprisingly, I fell into the standard male pattern of being "wowed by 'movie star' good looks, and appreciating women with 'traditional' or 'mainstream' appeal." Well, sure. The relevant question is whether I can look past my unrealistic fantasies to go out with "normal" attractive women, and the answer is an unequivocal *yes*.

But if I consider myself one of the enlightened guys out there—the ones who prefer the company of thirty-three-year-old women to twenty-three-year-old women because the older women are *so much more interesting*—then what about the legions of men out there who fit the worst male stereotypes? Stereotypes, which, after all, weren't manufactured by a bitter woman in a lab in Antarctica but, rather, have been reinforced by male Neanderthals for eons.

Listen, I wish it weren't true. I wish that I could report that there are a vast number of men out there who really don't care about how women look. I wish I could say that there are thousands of men e-mailing me each week wondering where they can find some quality women—ones with strong opinions, fascinating careers, and rapier wits. But there aren't.

I am not suggesting that men are pure objects of lust with all the depth of a bathtub. Nor am I suggesting that men don't have the ability to love and accept any physical imperfections. They can and they do.

Just not as much as women. At least in my experience as a consultant for online daters where I have the unique privilege of being given access to some of my clients' online dating accounts. And after years of doing this, I'm still flabbergasted that no matter how unattractive a man is—no matter how little hair is on his head or how much on his back—he *still* has the same twentysomething supermodels on his favorites list as if he was Colin Farrell.

Yes, Shallow Hal lives—and I believe he lives in a majority of American men. Men who are 5s want women who are 10s. And women who are 5s are often left out in the cold, at least in L.A. where I live. No doubt there are superior cities to this one, but I have to think a whiff of this epidemic has blown eastward.

I hope it's obvious that we're not bringing this up to pass judgment on women. In fact, if anybody should be judged harshly, it's men for refusing to let women age gracefully.

Most men do not break out of gender roles and societal expectations. So while you may know a handful of men who don't care about looks, they are rarities. They are the gold standard, the type that every woman should be striving to date. But if you're under the illusion that they grow on trees, it's time to wake up and smell the Kiehl's antiaging lotion. The number of guys who are "above" the whole looks thing may fill a classroom, but not a stadium and definitely not a big enough portion of the male population to suggest any type of trend.

In a weak moment, I bet that even the most nonjudgmental

guy around would say that he wants a mind, soul, and body connection—but only if she takes care of her body.

Linda

You can't grow up female, particularly in the United States or any other country in which *Baywatch* is shown, without getting the message that men would rather you were thin and beautiful and firm and smooth-skinned and tan and tall and glowing with pixie dust because you are possessed of the genetically unlikely combination of (1) teeny waist, (2) compact little ass, and (3) enormous, perfectly spherical breasts. I don't think anyone can claim that we don't know the score.

Women who don't fit the classic definition of beauty figure it out during childhood, and if they're not careful, it burrows into their heads. It's like when you can't get yourself to stop singing "It's a Small World," only instead of lasting three days, it lasts twenty years. It's not a matter of not knowing how much men care about looks. That's not the issue.

What is an issue is harping on attention to physical attractiveness as if it is a character flaw either in a particular guy or in guys in general, which it isn't. Indeed, a smart woman doesn't stand around waiting for a man who will "forget" looks and care only about her true self, because *everyone cares about looks, including women*. In fact, I have often secretly suspected that women who snort derisively that it's undignified to care about looks have spent their lives around men who are smart and homely, and when they meet one who's blisteringly hot but jaw-droppingly stupid, they're going to feel pretty silly standing there trying to look casual and not choke on the smoke rising off their own underwear.

This is not to say you have to be that *Baywatch* ideal or resign yourself to life alone. The average woman is, by definition, average-looking, and people date her and sleep with her and fall in love with her and marry her. And some of those guys who genuinely can't cope with what natural breasts look like or how women age? Those are guys you don't want to date anyway until they grow up a little—even if they're in their fifties. The point is to find a peaceful spot to settle into where you're realistic about the fact that looks are always in the mix, but you're not tying yourself into knots over every imperfection.

There's something else, too, that shouldn't go unsaid. It's a little hackneyed to attribute subconscious motives to everything, but the women who are noisiest about having no interest in changing their appearance because they want someone to see beyond the surface and love them for what's in their hearts would be well advised to look themselves in the eye—hard, when they're really ready—and ask this question: *Are you intentionally using your looks to keep men away from you?* It sounds like something nobody would do in light of the harsh punishments meted out to women who don't fit the mold, until you begin to count up the number of weird mechanisms people have to control who gets close to them.

I mean, let's be honest. If you're a woman, you can assure yourself a lot of lonely, secure, low-risk solitude, if that's what you consciously *or* subconsciously want, by saying, with the way you look, that you don't give a damn. I'm saying it's something to consider. And if you're warming up to tell me that you refuse to sacrifice your individuality to meet some societal standard of blah blah blah, consider why wearing clothes that fit you or combing your hair is a threat to your individuality. Would you not be you anymore if you were thinner or better dressed? Because that's a problem, if that's what you think.

This isn't meant to be glib in some hippy-dippy "just decide you want to be beautiful and you will be" sense. But in the end, if this is the game you're playing, it isn't fair to be pissed off about the fact that your chosen method of isolating yourself is working because nobody has the patience to run the obstacle course and drag you kicking and screaming out of your tower of pain. That's not anybody's job; it's really not. And it will not, in the vast majority of cases, *ever* happen. Trust me, any weapon you pick up to drive other people off will probably work. Don't want to sit around by yourself? The Tower of Pain is probably pretty fuckin' tall by now, so look for the first set of stairs labeled DOWN and get moving.

Whatever you decide to do, don't expect to escape the fact that physicality is reality. It's not all of reality, but it's a big piece. You do not grow out of it, you do not rise above it, you do not teach yourself to ignore it, you do not squelch it, and you will never beat it. So speak softly and, you know, carry a fire extinguisher.

2

Who Are You and What Did You Do with My Girlfriend?

Sex with the same person is going to get old no matter how attracted you are. All you can do is take special care to be creative in your dress, your technique, and your attitude.

Evan

Stop me if this sounds familiar: It's twelve o'clock on a Saturday night, dinner's over, drinks are over, the good *SNL* sketches are over, and you haven't had sex in at least a week. Feeling frisky, you kiss him, he removes your clothes, fondles your breasts, and goes down on you. You return the favor and then make love, going from missionary, to you on top, to doggie-style. He lasts for fifteen minutes. You come twice. You even snuggle afterward.

From what you've heard from your friends about their two-minute husbands who couldn't find their clitorises with a GPS, you should be pretty darned happy with your boyfriend's performance. But you're not. Truth be told, you could probably recite his moves in bed as sure as a commuter could recite his lineup of train stops. You know you're lucky. You know he's amazing. But a steak can be amazing, too, and you wouldn't want to have one of those every night for the rest of your life. And while you know you don't want to cheat, you've *gotta* shake things up a little bit.

Good news: he's probably on the same page as you. He still remembers why he's attracted to you, but, if pressed, he'd likely agree that the routine has gotten a little too, well, routine. More good news: he's a guy. Do you know how easy we are to please? No, really, do you? Figuring out what makes you tick requires a team of Japanese scientists and a Swiss mathematician, to boot. Getting us off takes a few fake screams. Maybe something on sale from Victoria's Secret that you sort of thought was pretty anyway. How lucky are you? Not so lucky? Boyfriend still not delivering the goods? Yeah. We hear ya. And since we're so sensitive to your plight, and a little offended that you'd even consider faking pleasure for our benefit, we would really, truly, honestly like to give you what you want.

That means *you have to tell us what you want.* And not just in the heat of the moment with an exasperated sigh and a tap of a ruler on the back of the head. But in a real discussion, before or after we have sex, where you can share your fantasies, without repercussion. Bringing things up spontaneously in bed can work, but keep in mind, it's pretty hard for us to recover when you whip out that 24-inch King Dong you ordered from Adam and Eve. Especially if we're not prepared for it. If you've ever had a boyfriend surprise you with anything big and plastic, you can probably understand.

But whether it's a little dirty talk whispered in our ears when we're having sex, a new position that you got out of *Cosmo,* or a late-night booty call wearing nothing more than a trench coat and pumps (you, not us), there are always things you can do to spice things up without creating any major waves. (Note: Inviting a third party into the bedroom is exciting, unforgettable, and a total recipe for disaster unless you are emotionally prepared to open up Pandora's box.) Better yet, stick to role-playing. Fantasies are fun, and while Naughty Nurse and Fuck-Me Fireman may not play out like your dreamy DVD scenarios, at least you won't destroy a lifetime of trust for a few jollies.

Regarding fantasies, one thing that is rarely acknowledged, or even believed, by women is that guys can get a little shy about sharing this sort of stuff. Just because we think about sex once every eight seconds doesn't mean we've ever thought of it in, like, a cerebral manner. So if you truly want a better sex life, you may have to take the lead, by letting him see your inner freak first. As long as it's not inspired by an *SNL* skit, which could be pretty weird.

Linda

The sad thing is the number of you who are right now considering running to Google in an attempt to track down Evan, the guy who says that during routine, boring sex you get to come twice.

You're going to get into a routine. And it's as true with sex as it is with everything else that no person is hot in quite the same way as a new person. New people make you sweat. They make you swoon, and you feel drunk on them, really. Yes, there are people who will tell you that their spouses still make them swoon after thirty years, blah blah, but if they tell you it's in exactly the same way, they're lying. But if you're starting to feel overly choreographed, like some kind of naked Busby Berkeley musical, you don't have to settle for that, and you shouldn't. The same comfort level that can lead to monotony ought to also give you the space to try something, or talk about something, that maybe would be a little much for a guy you just met. It's a good thing. It's a promising thing. Whatever you've been hiding in a box under the bed, figuratively or literally, there's no time like the present to haul it out.

This doesn't mean all new ideas are good ideas, of course. Despite its ubiquity as a fantasy for men and women both, the third-party business simply has an incredibly shitty track record among people who have tried it as a way to spice up an ongoing two-person relationship—as opposed to people who specifically dig polyamory or whatever, and to those people, honestly, knock yourselves out, but we're not writing that book (*Why You're Still Merely Double* or something).

What it does mean is that once you're comfortable, you're just going to have to talk, even in situations where it's not easy. While you have undoubtedly had occasion to discuss most common topics (politics, religion, fast-food restaurants) with people often enough to gauge how common your preferences are, you probably have not had the same opportunities with regard to your preferences about sex. So you have no idea what the odds are that, if you just give it time and give the equivalent of the Siskel and Ebert thumbs-up/thumbs-down to what you're being offered, your boyfriend will magically and eventually hit upon whatever your particular cork popper is. *If I wait around long enough,* you think to yourself, *he will see that I have a lot of neckties in my closet for a woman, and this light will go on* . . . and it really won't. Or if it does, it will take a lot longer than it would if you just said, "Let me tell you about the first time I saw *Working Girl,*" and take it from there.

And can we talk for a moment, a little tangentially, about faking it, another bad idea? What the hell? That's like writing on the customer satisfaction card at the B&B, "Yes, I *loved* the blueberry muffins!" when, in fact, the basket of hockey pucks got tossed into the trash, forcing you to sneak out later and buy *yourself* the eggs Benedict you really wanted, if you see my point. Don't do that, at least not regularly. That's a maneuver specifically calculated to perpetuate your state of dissatisfaction. (That's not to be confused, of course, with souping up the drama of your genuine response, which can be an entirely appropriate, go-team act of generosity and encouragement.)

Afraid of hurting his feelings? Yeah, okay. But if you're afraid to tell the guy to touch this instead of that, you probably shouldn't be having sex with him in the first place—and in this context, we're talking about relationships, really, and at that point? Yeah, you've got to be willing to have that talk.

3

Good Girls Don't

Nobody's ever gone to hell for enjoying sex, or gone to heaven for being all "Oh, all right" about it, or perpetuating the myth that sex from a woman is a favor. Don't play that game; own what you want. Your grandmother isn't looking.

Evan

When it comes to sex—especially sex with someone new—men can be hypocritical morons. They think about sex, they talk about sex, they push you into sex, and then they judge you for having sex. That's not just unfair, it's patently awful—like a dentist offering you a candy bar and dropping you as a patient for eating it. You can't let it paralyze you, but you can't ignore that it's real.

Somehow, a large percentage of men have been unable to logically resolve this paradox, which condemns anyone who gives them exactly what they're asking for. In essence, it's sort of a test, except unlike most tests, men don't even know they're testing you. But if you wanna really get to the bottom of what makes guys tick, consider this little nugget: men want to feel special. It's not that you slept with him on the second date that bothers him; it's the thought that maybe you sleep with *every* guy on the second date. That would explain the big deal about men's virgin fantasies. Men want to go where no man has gone before—at least not that many of 'em—if only because it makes them feel bigger and, well, special.

Still, there's no point in denying that you are a sexual being with desires as frequent, and frequently kinky, as the men you desire. Men are fickle over the littlest things when it comes to sex and can sometimes get uncomfortable when you let it all hang out right away. In the same way that men choose to believe that women don't fart even though they know the truth, they also choose to believe that their woman has never been down and dirty with another guy—much less a bunch of other guys—over a series of many years. It's a truth that may exist in your former life, but we'd rather not know about it in the present.

Within the context of a trusting relationship, however, you should toss all those calculated poses out the window. Once you're with a guy, it's in everybody's best interest if you are able to unleash your inner porn star. While we can be big talkers, we still take our cues from our environment. Which is to say that the only way we know about sex is from reading about it, watching it, or experiencing it. That's where you need to step up. It's not about doling out sex at regularly scheduled intervals or pursing your lips when he suggests a new position. It's about being "GGG—good, giving, and game," as sex columnist Dan Savage points out. It's about letting him know what *you* want, so he can give it to you in a way that leaves you genuinely satisfied. Men are an achievement-oriented gender, and your orgasms are little gold stars for our notebooks. As anyone who's ever faked it knows, we get off on you getting off. Isn't it about time you got off for real?

So, for any women who want more than theory and are looking for a rule that will appeal to all men in the bedroom, here you go, on the house: When in doubt in the bedroom, say *yes*. Except if he asks you if you've ever tried that kinky thing before with someone else—then the answer's always *no*.

Linda

Nothing makes Hollywood happier than punishing trollops. Of the four nitwits on *Sex and the City*, which one got cancer? The slut.

Of the many pinheads on *Dawson's Creek,* which one died of a nonspecific heart ailment? The slut. Virgins gone astray are generally treated similarly. When a young woman in a television drama decides to have sex, particularly for the first time, she will either get pregnant or believe she's pregnant, even if she uses multiple forms of birth control and keeps her clothes on the entire time.

It shouldn't be that hard, of course, to avoid this kind of terrible fate, because popular wisdom will tell you that women don't like sex anyway, at least not for its own sake. We only like the closeness, right? We only like it when we get flowers. It stands to reason under this theory that women aren't capable of enjoying casual sex, because the only women who enjoy sex recreationally are the ones who have been abused or are afraid of love or are using sex for power and so forth.

The same rule applies when we're in relationships, according to the famous Ann Landers column announcing that she had conducted a survey showing that women don't specifically crave sex at all, but are happy with what she adorably referred to as cuddling. One could hope that "cuddling" was a cloying euphemism encompassing everything short of intercourse, in which case you could twist it into something that had some validity, within reason, sort of. But the way it was interpreted was that women don't really care about the sweaty, grabby, orgasm business—we just want to kind of lie around and . . . read poems? I'm not even sure.

Indeed, the cultural baggage associated with women's enjoyment of sex is enough to sink a freighter. And the potential problems it creates are equally oppressive. It certainly condemns women who have enjoyed sex outside serious relationships, because according to this theory, they are—you guessed it—sluts. They must be confused. They hate themselves. No self-esteem. Time for that mysterious but fatal condition!

Look, as for all the theories that women can't ever separate sex and emotional closeness, I'm not a biologist, and I'm not going to tell you whether or not women are chemically programmed to spontaneously start using the word "boyfriend" after sex. It certainly hasn't been my experience that that's the case, but it may be for some people. What's so dangerous about this entire dynamic, however, is that it makes women—not all women, but some women—feel guilty and weird about admitting or talking about the fact that they enjoy sex, at least sometimes, for its own sake. Not because they feel cared about or cherished or bonded to anyone, but just because it's hot and good and fun. Which, no matter what Ann Landers said, does indeed occur.

Losing track of that fact has the potential to throw women badly off-course, because it prevents them from telling their partners what they want in bed, because they're not supposed to care about the actual sex part anyway. Furthermore, and maybe most relevant to the questions we're asking in this book, it seems to sometimes have the unfortunate effect in relationships of setting up a strange and cyclic dynamic in which sex is a favor given by women and received by men.

Don't get me wrong, the vast majority of relationships don't work this way. But you can see how it would happen. If you were to buy the idea that women just need cuddling, and really just want bonding, then sex itself is more for the guy than it is for her. This is how women get grudging and stingy about sex, an attitude to which men often respond by looking at it purely as a vehicle for their own satisfaction. Which makes it worse for the woman, and the cycle repeats itself. Holding out as punishment, doling it out at a given point in the relationship based on whether the guy will lose respect for you—these are maneuvers that are based on the idea that you hand out sex like candy at Christmas, as a favor. It's a very, very bad idea.

I'm certainly not suggesting that you drain what's intimate and personal out of your sex life; that isn't the point. Nor am I suggesting that you pretend sex has no potential consequences, emotional or otherwise, because it obviously does, and ignoring them is a great way to ruin your life. What I'm suggesting is only that you be aware of, and stay away from, the cultural bullshit that instructs you that, in all cases, (1) there's something amiss in your psyche if you want sex, (2) you're going to hell if you enjoy it for its own sake, or (3) you shouldn't need it if you're getting enough hugs. Ugh. It's totally appropriate for you to want it, and for you to expect to enjoy it, and it doesn't have to be about getting flowers. Of course, there are loaded reasons why some women have lots and lots of sex; there are also loaded reasons why some women don't. What matters is that once you're an adult, you should act according to your own timetable and your own judgment and get every voice in your head that isn't your own to shut the hell up.

PART VIII

You're Missing the Signals for When to Get Out . . . and When to Stick Around

Deal Breakers

Rose-Colored Glasses Don't Actually
Make the World Rosy

Disciples, Acolytes, and Other
Unequal Partners

Hitting on 20

1

Deal Breakers

When there are real problems that you're trying to sweep under the rug, you should face them head-on or get out. You aren't doing yourself or anyone else a favor by pretending you can live with what you can't.

Evan

As a woman, you probably want a man who is tall, dark, and handsome; a man who is financially secure and family oriented; and a man who can build a deck, play guitar, and make love all night. Assuming such a man actually exists on this earthly plane, (a) he may not find you as fascinating as he finds himself, (b) he probably has a considerable number of other dating options, and (c) he may make racist jokes, hate his mother, and boss you around mercilessly. In other words, even the perfect man isn't perfect, so don't worry so much about finding him. It's more important to figure out what traits and qualities you can and cannot tolerate in a man for the rest of your life.

Let's run down some of the big ones, broken up into a few major categories:

Vices: Smoking, Drinking, Drugs

Vices are reasonable deal breakers provided that one or more of the parties is at the far end of the "I do/I don't" spectrum. Someone who puts "bong hits" on his daily to-do list will probably not mesh well with a Nancy Reagan type. A woman in AA may be better served with a teetotaling partner as opposed to a boozing

Wall Street guy. In most instances, however, people are way too in-
tolerant of their partners' vices. If she's not into porn, what's the difference if he hops online and spends a half-hour surfing for things
he's too embarrassed to discuss? As long as everything is consumed
in moderation and in such a way that doesn't impact our day-to-
day lives, what's the point of making moralistic judgments?

Values and Tastes: Movies, Music, Politics, Religion

You like *Free Willy,* he likes *Scarface.*

You like Eminem, he likes Tim McGraw.

You like Sondheim, he likes A-Rod.

You crazy kids should stay together. While it's nice to share this
kind of stuff, it's hardly imperative. Art and culture is the perfect
arena to learn to compromise because the stakes are so very low.
On the other hand . . .

You contributed to the Dean campaign, he has a Bush bumper
sticker on the back of his SUV.

You want to bring the kids to church on Sundays, he wants to
schlep them to temple on Fridays.

You like the stability of monogamy, he likes the variety of
polyamory.

You might want to rethink your relationship. Big issues can become wedges in your relationship, and you may forever resent not
having a partner who sees eye to eye with you on the important
stuff. And yes, there are plenty of exceptions, so cool it if you
come from a proud Republican/Democrat or Jewish/Christian
household. I'm just saying it's more difficult, that's all.

Physical Shortcomings: Height, Weight, Age, Hair

It's tough to get on people's cases about attraction. It's either
there or it isn't. It's just a shame when people have such lofty stan-
dards of beauty that 98 percent of people don't even qualify.

(Ahem. . . .) This is an epidemic with men as we've discussed. Women, to their credit, are more forgiving of men's paunches and shiny domes, but I'm still struck by the emphasis they put on height. When asked about it, they'll say things like, "I just want a man who is bigger than me, someone who makes me feel protected." From what?! Falling anvils? Stampeding elephants? Warring tribes? Honestly, unless a guy is painting a wall or taking down dishes, his height serves no purpose whatsoever to your happiness or survival. So, if you're under five-foot-four, then please cut the five-foot-seven guys a little bit of slack, will ya?

Money, Money, Money, Money

I recently went to a fascinating dating/relationships seminar run by a very bright woman named Alison Armstrong. A quick poll of the women in attendance shockingly revealed that, given the option, a majority would quit work and become full-time homemakers. Another large portion wanted to keep their careers but admitted that they'd like to have the option of staying at home. Now this wasn't some sort of Turn-Back-the-Clock, fifties Renaissance Club. This was a ballroom at a hotel in downtown Los Angeles filled with successful women in their thirties and forties. What wasn't mentioned in this seminar, however, was how unrealistic these desires were. In order for a woman to stay at home, raise and educate two kids, and maintain her lifestyle, complete with occasional shopping and vacations, her husband would have to make a salary in the 90th percentile of Americans (a figure that I completely made up, by the way). This is not to say that this traditional domestic arrangement cannot and will not happen; it does all the time. I just think it bears mentioning that nine out of ten guys are going to fall short of making that kind of living.

So while there's nothing wrong with desiring financial stablity, realize that if you dream of staying home to raise a family, you'd better find a very successful man to support you. And even if this whole stay-at-home concept doesn't apply to you at all, don't kid yourself. Money matters more than any of us would like to admit. Out of all deal breakers, it is the most common cause of divorce. Do yourself a favor right now and assess how important money is to you. It's not wrong to be conscious of it, and perhaps you can avoid breaking a middle-class guy's heart somewhere down the road.

Linda

You have a list, probably, of the things you won't live with. Maybe it's smoking, maybe it's people who are sanctimonious about smoking, maybe it's people who watch TV, maybe it's people who think less of you because you watch *Judge Judy*. Serious things like people with kids, frivolous things like people with fish—everybody has a list. And everybody has thrown it away at least once.

I mean, sure. You don't sleep with Republicans. Except *that one*, and he's really just a fiscal conservative, right? And you don't date short guys, unless they're tall in spirit. Everybody's done it. Lists are just lists, and they're theoretical constructs more than anything. If you're lucky, the guys you wind up being crazy about are ones where . . . you wouldn't have imagined them, because you *couldn't* have imagined them, exactly. Things that annoy you in most people work for other people, because a guy's personality is more like a big tangle of string than like a bag of marbles where each one stands for a particular quality.

So I'm all in favor of reconsidering your list, because some things that look nonnegotiable turn out to have asterisks next to them. The problem is that some things actually are nonnegotiable. You do have limits. Everybody does.

It would be great if all those limits were merit based, wouldn't it? It would be great if anything that was so serious that you couldn't overcome it would also be so serious that you would walk away without any regrets. Of course, if that were the case, there wouldn't be so many people staying in relationships in which they clearly cannot be happy. Black and white are nice colors in which to live your life, but you don't see much of them after the seventh grade. What really, royally sucks is the guy who's absolutely right for you in every way except the one that you can't get over and aren't going to.

We've talked a lot about why people avoid conflict—fear, inertia, worry that they'll never find anyone else . . . it really doesn't matter. There are a lot of reasons people refuse to acknowledge problems they probably know at some level are not ones they can either solve or learn to live with. What does matter is that you recognize that there are three things to do with a problem in your relationship or with the person you're in the relationship with. There's (1) tackling it (which can be a long-term process), (2) learning to live with it (give or take occasional non-life-threatening expressions of frustration), and (3) finding somebody else. Those are the only three choices you have. Go ahead, name your fourth choice.

Yeah, I didn't think so. Once you know those are the only three options, you can learn quite a bit. If you're (1) not going to solve it and (2) unwilling to live with it, you'll have to (3) find somebody else. If you (1) can't solve it, but you're (3) not willing to end the relationship, you'll have to (2) get over it. If you can't (2) get over it, and you're pretty sure you don't want to (3) find somebody else, then guess what? You're going to have to (1) tackle it.

And when you're out of options, you're out of options. It happens, even between really good people who have a lot going for them. There are easy ones you can name all day long—if you really want kids and the guy really doesn't want kids, then what are you going to do? It's not really something you can fix, and it's not something where I'd recommend either one of you accepting an outcome other than the one you want, because living with it doesn't just mean *agreeing* to live with it. It means actually *living* with it, and doing it without holding a grudge. Grudges are poisonous. Do you have some old, stale issue you bring up all the time? Then you're not living with it. And you're certainly not solving it. See where I'm going with this?

When you're dealing with a particularly thorny issue, you're not doing anything good for yourself, and you're certainly not doing anything good for anyone else, by stubbornly standing with feet and hands all over different parts of the board like you're playing Twister—this hand is on Let It Go, that foot is on Break Up, this hand is on Have Another Serious Talk. Pick something. Do it. Take it seriously. What you can't live with, you can't live with, and that doesn't make you a bad person. It's certainly not any worse to realize after a month that you don't want to date a guy who goes out with his friends every weekend and end the relationship than it is to admit it only after a year or two of suffering by all concerned.

You have a list; everybody has a list. You shouldn't be afraid to ignore it when the time calls for it, but you shouldn't throw it out, either. Because it's still yours, whether you carry it in your pocket or stuff it under the mattress.

2

Rose-Colored Glasses Don't Actually Make the World Rosy

The people who love you are going to bring you a lot of happiness, but they won't fix everything that's wrong. If you expect to be perfectly happy all the time, then you're guaranteeing disappointment before you even start.

Evan

Grandpa died at age sixty-nine in 1987. His last letter to me, written when I was in summer camp, was eerily deep and prescient for a healthy guy who died of a sudden heart attack. In it, he gave me some words of wisdom, which I'm going to pass along to you. If you live by them, great. If you can tell me how to live by them, I owe you a drink.

> *"No one is ever really happy. The main thing is not being unhappy. Be content and you'll never be unhappy."*

Easier said than done, but finding that middle ground between manic and depressive is an absolute necessity. Life will always throw you for a loop, because that's what life does, and if you get thrown out of the saddle instantly, you'll never experience the full ride. Recognize that the glass can *always* be seen as half-empty and that, even at its best, love hurts. Whatever joy you feel when things are at their best is no greater than the pain you feel when things are falling apart. Still, even when things are humming along, finding a partner doesn't magically fill up your emptiness; it just allows you to share it with someone.

You've heard it before, but I'm obliged to repeat it again: Happiness does not begin with a husband. It may continue, deepen, and build, but a man alone can't make you happy. He'll certainly try. He can say it's his pleasure, he can say it's his privilege, but whether he'll tell you this or not—*it's not his job*. Happiness, like loneliness, is a temporary state of mind, when things seem to be clicking on all cylinders and you're not paying any mind to the empty part of the glass. So you got a raise, lost six pounds, bought a cute handbag, had dinner with the girls, and feel *soooo* lucky to be with this amazing guy. Then tomorrow, you get stuck in traffic, get reprimanded by your boss, stain your pants, eat takeout alone, and find out that your guy has to work until eleven and can't make it over. That's a bad day. But it's not a bad life, and it doesn't erase all the good stuff that you still have going for you. It just temporarily obscures it.

All the affection, warmth, sex, and companionship in the world cannot make an unhappy person into a happy person. That's why striving for contentment—refusing to let the highs get too high or the lows get too low—better equips you to ride the waves of love, without getting nauseous.

Linda

It's a profound understatement to say that happiness is really difficult. And much of the time, it's not so much that you can't visualize it as it is that there's always something between it and you. The problem you have to solve, the thing you have to take care of, the person you're hoping will call (or won't call) or will go away (or won't go away). The chase can be so frustrating that it's easy to get very "if only" about it. *If only* you had this, *if only* you had that, and, especially, *if only* you could meet somebody really good.

But it's depressing as hell to end up looking at your life like it's an outline drawing in a coloring book, as if you're supposed to go through and color inside all the lines and wind up with something that's completed in some way. It's not a zero-sum game; how much happiness you have isn't defined by how much unhappiness you can get rid of. Those things that stand between you and your vision of a perfect life—that thing you have to take care of, that problem you have to solve, the big question you haven't answered—they're still out there, whether you're single or not.

It's not that I dismiss the profound impact that relationships with other people have on your general level of contentment. When somebody you're really crazy about spins you into that fragile little happy cocoon where everything temporarily *feels* fixed just because of the way it feels to have him breathe in your ear, that's no small thing. Don't believe anybody who tells you it's entirely about happiness from within. Other people matter; giving up on that doesn't make you a realist so much as a sociopath.

The problem comes if you're anticipating finding someone who's going to come in all *date ex machina*, fixing everything that's amiss and righting a million wrongs. Because when that doesn't happen—and it won't—you're going to feel like this must not be the person for you. It's a good way to talk yourself out of something that might otherwise make you happy.

Besides, looking for *all* your happiness in other people isn't even strategically smart. People who aren't interested in their own lives are boring. I remember being out once with a very nice guy who literally had nothing to say about his life. He enjoyed talking about me, enjoyed talking about what I did, enjoyed asking me lots of questions about it, but when asked about his own life, he could only dismiss his job as meaningless and tell me he had no idea what else he might want to do instead. I'm not talking about the struggling artist who finds humor in stories about life at the frozen-french-fry factory; that's a different issue. You don't have to love everything you're doing right this minute. But you have to basically like your life, or you're not going to attract anyone worth meeting.

Happiness isn't a fixed point anyway. You find it; you fumble it. You get and you give as much as you can as often as you can, and that's the best you're going to do. So when you get spun into that happy little cocoon, try to get a few uninterrupted breaths of the air in there, because it's not always easy to find your way to that place. You can't stay in there all day, but it doesn't mean you should go jumping out.

3

Disciples, Acolytes, and Other Unequal Partners

Everyone wants respect; everyone wants love. But worship is actually toxic. Hooking yourself to a guy who's going to idolize and idealize you is not as pleasant as it sounds.

Evan

Much of this book is dedicated to the analysis of our flaws and how to deal with them in the context of a relationship. My guess is that the perfect people just skimmed that part until they got to this chapter. Welcome, Greek gods. Now hang up your togas and tell your disciples to sit quietly in the back where they belong.

For many years, I thought that there was only one woman for me. She was one of those people that every guy had a crush on—cute, smart, witty, generous, silly—and every other praiseworthy adjective out there. We had a little game for years where I wouldn't be able to hang up the phone until I complimented her three times. I thought it was all in good fun and only later noticed the obvious pathology behind it. In my mind, my heaps of praise were merely a means to express my affection and win her over. She, in turn, liked to hear my kind words because they made her feel good. What my excessive flattery wasn't supposed to do was to have an equally chilling effect on her. See, because of my kiss-ass behavior, she didn't think that she'd ever be good enough for me. She thought that when I discovered the "truth" about her, I could only be disappointed. In actuality, I knew exactly what her problems were; I just chose to focus on the positive. But that doesn't matter. My perception was wrong, and her perception was the reality. And in reality, the moment I became her fan, I ceased being a man.

I have a few friends whose wives seem less like equal partners than mothers, daughters, and starry-eyed admirers. I don't know what to make of this except to observe that all parties actually seem . . . happy. She found her father figure; he found his 24/7 fan club. Their basic needs are fulfilled, and who am I to tell them they're incorrect? But this chapter is about the reverse situation, where you're the object of desire—the figurative rock star to that groupie you call your boyfriend. Hey, it certainly beats the alternative. Having your own personal sycophant answering to your every whim is a far cry from the other extreme, which, I'm told, involves lots of alcohol, extramarital sex, and repeated mentions of the word "bitch." Still, neither end of the acolyte seesaw seems to be all that rewarding. Isn't mutual respect the underpinning of every relationship, whether it's work or pleasure? Can you truly respect a guy who is merely a vessel for your happiness and has no other raison d'être?

I've got this theory that I've been floating for years. I generally bring it up when asked what kind of woman I want to marry. The word "respect" always seems to creep into most people's descriptions. Not me. I'm aiming higher. The woman I marry has to be someone that I *admire*; someone who I can say, with every ounce of confidence, is the best person I've ever known. But not in the unhealthy way. I don't think she's perfect. The reason the relationship works is because she feels the same way about me. They call it a mutual admiration society. The great thing about it is that you only need two members and you're set. If you look around and discover you're the only member, you should probably keep recruiting.

Linda

A friend of mine used to say that one of the snags in any relationship is that, at any given moment, someone's winning and someone's losing. He didn't believe in complete parity: somebody is always a little more into it; somebody is always a little more sure; somebody always needs it a little more. The idea is that it isn't always the same person from one day to the next, but it's always someone. That person, according to this theory, is losing.

I suspect that much is probably, in an entirely cynical sense, true. It's awfully difficult to achieve a perfect balance of power, given that even if you do pull it off, it's probably impossible to maintain it for more than five minutes. It's as true in relationships as it is with anything else that—like the song says—sometimes you're the windshield, and sometimes you're the bug.

But when things are so skewed that it feels more like teacher/student . . . or star/fan . . . or even parent/child, well, I've seen a few of those, and they don't end well. I've known a couple of women who have found themselves the "winners" in relationships like this, where they're worshipped and bootlicked and sucked up to within an inch of their lives. There's a certain security in it, of course, because your odds of being left or cheated on or wronged drop dramatically when the guy you're with gets up every day just genuinely happy for the chance to pour you a cup of coffee.

As good as it sounds, though, to be admired, I've never known anyone who found it satisfying for very long. Admittedly, I don't get the appeal of the metaphor about being placed on a pedestal, anyway. Why do you want to be up there all by yourself? And aren't pedestals for statues? For prized and displayed *things,* rather than for people? Ask yourself whether anyone who idealizes you can possibly really know you. You're not perfect; you know this. You don't have superpowers, and you aren't made of cotton candy, and you don't smell like flowers after an hour at the gym. Anyone who doesn't know this doesn't know you. The same friend who told me about winning and losing also told me once that he believes that all people really want is to believe there's someone in the world who truly knows them. It's as good an explanation of bone-deep loneliness as I've ever heard.

And doesn't it make you wonder what's in it for him? Being with someone who's so very much better than he is? Some people become worshippers rather than partners because they're looking for a little glory to rub off on them. If you're the most beautiful woman in your social circle, he wants to be the most beautiful woman's boyfriend. He doesn't really want *you*; he just wants people to know you picked him. Some do it because your approval is worth more to them than anyone else's, and all they want is for you to give them the stroke that says they're worth something. Sound like insecurity? It is. As we've said over and over, insecurity is the irritating little punk-ass hiding behind most of the ugliness in relationships. This is no exception.

Do you really want to be a guy's reason for living? Can you stand up to that? Ironically, a guy who pulls this routine only *looks* like he's staring up at you. In reality, he's looking down at you from where he sits on your shoulders, crushing you under the weight of those demands. You cannot be anyone's universe. Even if you could, why would you want to? What would *he* be offering? The idea is to find someone with whom you can *share* your life, right? Not someone who can be tossed in like sugar into coffee and then be counted on to agreeably dissolve.

In the end, if the guy you're with believes that you're perfect, one of two things will happen. Either he will figure out that you're not, and that will hurt, or he will never figure out that you're not, meaning that even if your relationship is fifty years long, it will be an inch deep. Do yourself a favor and find a guy who could rattle off the three things he most digs about you, the three things about you that drive him the battiest, and the three things he's still figuring out. It doesn't mean he actually needs to tell you, but you should believe he could.

4

Hitting on 20

There's a reason you don't ask for another card when you have 20 in blackjack. It's because there's only a miniscule chance that you're going to beat the hand you already have. Recognize when your relationship is a 20 and when it's time to hold on to it instead of quitting for greener grass.

Evan

You've probably heard this story before:

Girl meets guy and knows, from their first kiss, that he's "the one." Meeting him, to her, is the equivalent of getting 20 in blackjack. He may not be perfect, but he's way closer than she's gotten before, and that's good enough. After a bit of soul-searching, she decides that this is going to be the man she marries. She's secure in her decision because she's gone out with so many men before and knows that catches like this are hard to find. Then, suddenly, he breaks up with her—even though he admits they had something special, even though he said he'd never loved a woman in his entire life the way he loved her.

What lingers with me when I hear this story is not whether the guy was telling the truth about his feelings for her, but whether breaking up will ultimately be the right move for him. This tale—experienced by most of us—brings up a very common dilemma. I call it the "You Just Know" syndrome.

In my mind, it takes nothing away from a perfectly happy couple to acknowledge that however much you might want to say "you just know," when a relationship is right you *never* just know. You can't. Life is too unpredictable and has far too many variables. Infidelity, boredom, financial ruin, and physical decline have all been known to split up couples that have taken eternal vows. For many people, it's not which of these things might happen, it's which of these things might *not* happen. And still, for all the crap that life throws our way, somehow, 50 percent of marriages manage to survive. That's an amazing statistic right there.

My parents were married for thirty years before my dad passed away. When I was young, I asked each of them independently how they knew that they were meant to be together. Not surprisingly, neither of them knew for sure. Well, how could they? He was twenty-three and she was twenty-two when they got hitched. They didn't know much of anything. And had Mom determined at some point that she was better off alone, or Dad felt that they married too young and needed to experience other people, this would be just another story of another suburban divorce.

The point is that my parents made it, but they didn't have to. They had no idea what the next thirty years had in store for them when they said, "I do." All they did was believe in the sanctity of their commitment, and they found a way to make it work.

I believe in love and lifetime partnerships and all that. I just can't shake the idea that with any permanent contract into which you voluntarily enter, you're going to have second thoughts. It's smart to go in with a full awareness of what a fifty-year commitment entails. If you don't think you're cut out for it, better to delay or bail than to go through the motions until you get the divorce that in your heart you knew was inevitable.

Will you ever know, beyond a shadow of a doubt, that you're meant to spend the rest of your life with one man? Probably not. But the next time you get 20 in blackjack, consider how long it took to pull that card and whether it's worth it to keep fishing for that ace.

Linda

I made the same New Year's resolution for about ten years in a row. Literally, I made it every January 1, over and over again. And I failed at it every year, until I ultimately gave up. It went like this: *I resolve to have at least 25 percent fewer feelings about everything.*

It might sound stupid, and weird, and doomed, but I meant well. I'd been flattened by my own swoony, impassioned, powerful reactions to things to the point where I made a very conscious decision to get brutally rational about everything. And when I decided to get brutally rational about myself, I had no shortage of theories—some goofy, some not. I had a handful of major revelations about some of my ill-advised choices, and, indeed, the frequency with which I made those stupid choices decreased. I made enormous improvements to my life on a bunch of different fronts, and it was absolutely the result of conscious effort, and good for me, right?

Right. Absolutely. But would you like to know how many feelings I have about things, compared to before? Yeah, it's about the same. Because no matter how smart you get, and no matter how carefully you think through exactly what you want, and no matter how hard you try to give your life rules, the way the Atkins diet or a solitaire game has rules, there are still going to be emotional, ethereal things going on that aren't going to entirely make sense. This, to me, is where the challenge lies in not letting a good relationship get away from you while, at the same time, not settling for less than you want.

Because, on the one hand, I agree with Evan. Of course, you never "just know." And people who think they're going to "just know" often wind up engaging in a lot of magical thinking and hunting for signs, like those people who think it means something that Lincoln's secretary was named Kennedy and Kennedy's secretary was named Lincoln. Hey, when I was young, I knew a guy with a heart-shaped birthmark. I know about this stuff. It's insane to expect that there's going to be some grand Presentation of the Romantic Fantasy—one that will lead you to absolute certainty that this is the person who's meant for you, and you for him, and you will never again doubt it. And you will never wonder if there's someone else out there, and you will never be attracted to anyone else, and you will never go through periods where you don't want to talk to him, or don't want to sleep with him, or don't feel like he gets you.

But, on the other hand . . . man, there's still a certain amount of alchemy involved. It's more than just the sum of the parts, where physical attraction plus good conversation plus shared values plus shared interests plus geographical and circumstantial practicality equals Congratulations, You Have Met the Right Person. I remember the first time I was with a guy and realized that just talking to him was giving me JELL-O knees. And realizing that it wasn't either a metaphor or a euphemism—that being "weak in the knees" was a real thing, and it's really your knees, and they're really weak. I'll be damned. You know what I did? I laughed. Out loud. Try explaining that one to somebody you don't know well yet. Total number of guys, out of all the ones I have ever met, who have had that effect on me: three. Three. Out of a whole damn lot. Are they the most physically attractive guys I've ever met? Nope. Are they the ones I've liked the most or connected with the best? Nope. Would it ever occur to me that that meant I should marry them? Nope. My point is only that there's an element of just . . . well, honestly, who in the hell knows?

You do have to be rational, and you have to think logically about what you want. I've already said a bunch of times in this book that you have to play the odds, and, believe me, I'm not just saying it. And more and more, in my own life, I actually do it. Do the math, choose to exit situations that are no-win, choose to pursue the ones with the best apparent prospects or the most upsides or the most happiness along the way, and eat the fact that some part of me is never sure I did the right thing. There's no certainty with other people, *ever*. Everybody is a calculated risk. You're always guessing, and you're always gambling. And you're still going to have to hit a little good luck and good timing, because that's how it goes.

Ultimately, you'll never reduce a relationship to a science or a statistics problem. The mistake is in believing you're waiting to stumble over some vaguely defined notion of romantic destiny when, in fact, you're hunting for mathematical certainty. You can have the weak knees, you can have the finishing each other's sentences, you can have that mystical and elusive whatever, and you still won't "know," if you expect to "know" the way you know your own name. Because being smart doesn't really mean having fewer feelings about everything; it means tempering them with a little perspective.

Acknowledgments

Evan Marc Katz would like to thank:

Lisa Hochberg, Daryl Katz, Tahra Millan, Jeff Munjack, and Leslie Sugel, for their insight and feedback on the extra-long first draft of this book. Also to Marci Etter, Deborah Sedghi, Leslie Shatum, and Stacey Tannenbaum, who received this book and really would have read it if I had given them more time before my deadline: My bad—I hope I can hit you up the next time around.

Lavinia Evans, for taking care of me and giving me a platform to say (mostly) whatever I want. Barron Ebenstein for being my best friend and sounding board on all things dating-related. Plus, he came up with the title of the book, for which I can never repay him.

Stephanie Lee, for long, funny, phone conversations and oh-so-cool Christmas gifts.

Hilary Redmon, for believing in this book from Day 1 and for making it palatable for readers every day afterward.

Mom. Always gotta thank my Mom.

Linda Holmes, for being the ideal friend and foil when writing *Why You're Still Single*. She's *so smart*, *so funny*, and *so crystal clear* in her metaphors that I can only say that I'm *so lucky* to call her my writing partner.

Every woman that I've ever dated. While the bad experiences make for funnier stories and better lessons learned, it's the good ones that assure me that happy, healthy relationships are possible. I wish the best for all of you, and I'm sorry about that one stupid thing that I did that one time. And all the other times, too.

Linda Holmes would like to thank:

My parents, for being enthusiastic fans, great company, and as much in love as ever.

Every English teacher I ever had. The Delaware Society of Professional Engineers, who threw an elegant banquet at which I accidentally dumped my plate in my lap at the age of fourteen, an experience that unquestionably made me the person I am today. Everyone who read the memoirs I wrote in eleventh grade. Dan Kelly, the first person to put me in print.

Sarah Bunting, Tara Ariano, and Dave Cole of Television Without Pity, for the writing job I had no idea I desperately wanted until they invented it. And everyone who ever wrote me an e-mail to tell me they laughed.

Stephanie Lee, for helping us figure out how to get this book written. Hilary Redmon, for editing it so brilliantly that it says what we meant.

My brilliant, indispensable friends, many of whom consulted on the book, talked to me about it, or listened to me talk about it: Jeff and Lora Alexander, John Ramos, Jeff Dybdahl, Ashley Horan, Sarah Leupen, Scott Alberts, Michael Bastedo, Amy Dunlap, Joshua Schiffman, Jason and Matthew Bribitzer-Stull, Elisabeth Klarqvist, and Joe Cox.

Stephen Thompson, my cherished friend, editor, and Music Stylist, for every note, every margarita, and especially every single word.

The inimitable Evan Marc Katz, for wanting to write this book, for wanting me to write it with him, and for being smart enough to write to me the second time when I was too dumb to write him back the first time.